D0743892

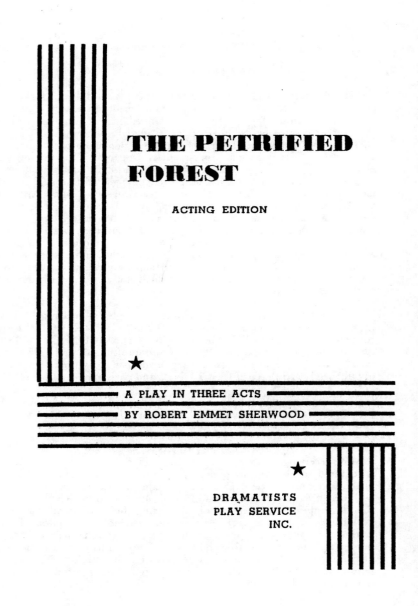

THE PETRIFIED FOREST

ACTING EDITION

A PLAY IN THREE ACTS

BY ROBERT EMMET SHERWOOD

DRAMATISTS
PLAY SERVICE
INC.

THE PETRIFIED FOREST
Copyright © Renewed 1961, 1962, Robert Emmet Sherwood
Copyright © 1934, 1935, Robert Emmet Sherwood

All Rights Reserved

To

MY MOTHER

THE PETRIFIED FOREST was first produced at the Broadhurst Theatre, New York City, by Gilbert Miller and Leslie Howard, in association with Arthur Hopkins, on January 7, 1935. Following is the original cast:

GRAMP MAPLE	Charles Dow Clark
BOZE HERTZLINGER	Frank Milan
A TELEGRAPH LINEMAN	Milo Boulton
ANOTHER LINEMAN	James Doody
JASON MAPLE	Walter Vonnegut
GABBY MAPLE	Peggy Conklin
PAULA	Esther Leeming
ALAN SQUIER	Leslie Howard
HERB	Robert Porterfield
MR. CHISHOLM	Robert Hudson
MRS. CHISHOLM	Blanche Sweet
JOSEPH	John Alexander
JACKIE	Ross Hertz
DUKE MANTEE	Humphrey Bogart
RUBY	Tom Fadden
PYLES	Slim Thompson
LEGION COMMANDER	Aloysius Cunningham
ANOTHER LEGIONNAIRE	Guy Conradi
SHERIFF	Frank Tweddell
A DEPUTY	Eugene Keith
ANOTHER DEPUTY	Harry Sherwin

Staged by Arthur Hopkins
Setting by Raymond Sovey

SCENE

The scene is the Black Mesa Bar-B-Q, gas station and lunch room at a lonely crossroads in the eastern Arizona desert.

The action begins late in the afternoon of an autumn day in 1934, and continues into the evening of the same day.

THE PETRIFIED FOREST

ACT I

*The scene of the entire play is the lunch room of the
Black Mesa Filling Station and Bar-B-Q on the desert in
Eastern Arizona.*

*There is an atmosphere about the place of strenuous if
not hearty welcome.*

*At the upper R. are double doors, with glass panels lead-
ing out to a covered porch. Off to the R., barely visible
through these doors, are the red pumps of the filling
station.*

*Downstage L. is a door leading to the bedrooms of the
MAPLE family who own this establishment. Upstage L.
is a swinging door leading to the kitchen. Upstage is a
lunch counter, with cash register, ketchup bottles, paper
napkins, toothpicks, chewing-gum and Life-Saver rack,
cigars, cigarettes, etc.*

*In the R. wall are wide windows, through which may be
seen the porch and, beyond it, the desert purpling in the
sunset. At the L. is a stove, with a high-backed rocking
chair beside it.*

*There are three small square tables—downstage L., down-
stage R. and C. There are three chairs at each table. At
the R., along the wall, is a wooden bench.*

*The walls are of phony adobe. The window and door
trimmings are painted a dark, burnt red. Above the
windows is a sign, with the words, "BLACK MESA
BAR-B-Q," worked in rustic letters. This formerly hung
outside, but was replaced by a Neon sign, the green
gleam of which will be evident later on when darkness
descends.*

*The walls are decorated with advertisements of Rye
Whiskey, Gas and Oil, the NRA, the TVA, the Red*

Cross, the American Legion, the Santa Fé R. R., Apache Beer, etc. On the wall is a framed photograph of General Pershing and below it an old service flag with one star. Prominently displayed is a crudely lettered sign that shouts: "TIPPING IS UN-AMERICAN—KEEP YOUR CHANGE!"

At the table downstage R. *are two* TELEGRAPH LINEMEN, *eating hamburger and drinking coffee. Both are young. The* FIRST *is thin and explosive in speech, the* SECOND *beefy and calm.*

Between them, and drawn back from the table, sits BOZE HERTZLINGER, *a stalwart, bronzed young man, who wears dirty white canvas pants and a filthy football jersey, on the back of which is a patch with the number 42. He is lighting a cigarette.*

At L. *in the rocking chair, sits* GRAMP MAPLE—*an old, old man. His eyes are watery and his vision blurred. His skin is like leather that has been dried by a lifetime under the desert sun and worn thin by constant rough usage. He holds a tattered pink copy of the Denver Post, but he is paying more attention to the talk of the* LINEMEN *than to the screaming headlines.*

1ST LINEMAN. (*Swallowing.*) Certainly it's Revolution! And that's exactly what we got to come to, whether a lot of old fluffs back east like it or not . . .

2ND LINEMAN. Yeah—and when it comes—how are *you* going to . . .

1ST LINEMAN. When it comes, we're going to finally get some of that equality they talked about in the Declaration of Independence.

2ND LINEMAN. Equality—hell! It's slavery. And how will you like that?

1ST LINEMAN. What have we got *now*, I'd like to know? Do you call *this* freedom? (*He stows more food into his nimble mouth.*)

BOZE. Listen to me, kid. In school we had to read up a lot on that cock-eyed system they got in Russia—and I'm here to tell you that if you were living over there you wouldn't be able to call your soul your own.

1ST LINEMAN. And how do I know I've *got* a soul?

BOZE. You're alive, aren't you?

6

1ST LINEMAN. Oh, sure—I'm alive. I got a heart—I can hear it beating. I got a stomach—I can hear it growling. I got blood—I can see it, when I stick myself with one of them God-damn splinters. But where's this soul that everybody hollers about?

BOZE. It's in your tongue, I guess. (*He winks broadly at* 2ND LINEMAN. *A car is heard stopping off at* R.)

1ST LINEMAN. Yeah—and maybe they got it locked up in the safe at the Postal Telegraph Company, along with the rest of their doubtful assets.

(JASON MAPLE *has come in from upper* R. *He is a dull, defeated man, of about forty, solemn, bespectacled, paunchy. He wears a gray alpaca cap, and a gray suit. In his lapel is an American Legion button.*)

JASON. (*To* BOZE.) Lady wants five gallons. Get going.

BOZE. O. K., boss. (*He pinches out the coal of his cigarette and places the butt behind his ear.*)

JASON. And you better keep on the alert out there so's customers don't have to wait. See?

BOZE. O. K., boss. (*He goes out.* 1ST LINEMAN *laughs.*)

1ST LINEMAN. And there's the guy who's here to tell me that in Russia you can't even call your soul your own.

JASON. You fellers want pie? (*His attitude toward* 1ST LINEMAN *is not conspicuously amiable.*)

2ND LINEMAN. Yeah.

1ST LINEMAN. And another cuppa coffee. (JASON *picks up their cups and goes to door at* L.) Rugged individualism! Every man for himself! That's the kind of liberty we've been getting.

JASON. (*Through door at the* L.) A couple of pies. (*He goes to coffee boiler on counter to refill the two cups.*)

2ND LINEMAN. What are you complaining about? You're eating.

1ST LINEMAN. (*Significantly.*) "Man cannot live by bread alone."

2ND LINEMAN. Who says he can't?

1ST LINEMAN. God says so! That's who.

2ND LINEMAN. Oh—is God a Russian?

1ST LINEMAN. He certainly ain't with the Postal Telegraph.

(PAULA, *the Mexican cook, comes in, bearing the pie.* JASON *lights a cigar.*)

JASON. Take these. (JASON *gives cups to* PAULA *as she passes.*)

7

1ST LINEMAN. Why do you suppose it is that Russia's got the whole world scared? It's because they're pushing ahead. They're pioneering!

GRAMP. They're what?

1ST LINEMAN. I said, they're pioneering. They're opening up new territory—and for the benefit of all, not so's a few land grabbers can step in and take the profits after somebody else has done the real work. Gracias. (*This is addressed to* PAULA, *who has delivered pie and is now removing remnants of the hamburger.*) Those engineers in Russia are building something new! That's where they've got it on us. We ain't building—we're *repairing.* Just like you and me. What do we do—day after day? We climb up poles, and fix the wires, so that some broker in New York can telegraph in a split second to some guy in Los Angeles to tell him he's ruined.

GRAMP. Well, my friend—when you talk about pioneering—you're talking about something I can tell *you* a few things about. (*He has risen and is crossing to occupy chair vacated by* BOZE.)

JASON. Shut up, Gramp.

GRAMP. I won't shut up.

JASON. I told you not to get into arguments with the guests.

GRAMP. Listen—I can tell these boys some things they'd be glad to hear. Wouldn't you, boys?

2ND LINEMAN. Sure! Go ahead, Pop. Change the subject. (*Both* LINEMEN *are devouring the pie.*)

GRAMP. Listen, my friend. I come down into this desert fifty-six years ago. I come down from Virginia City by way of Salt Lake and Mesa Verde. You had to be tough to cross this country in them days—Piyutes—Apaches—and plenty of white men with no love for their neighbors. Yes, *sir!* I was in your same line of business—wire-stringing. I helped string the first line that run west out of Albuquerque, and we had one hell of a time doing it, too.

(BOZE *comes in.*)

BOZE. Lady wants a pack of Camels.

GRAMP. Do you want to know who was the Governor of this territory in them days? Well, I'll tell you. General Lew Wallace. He wrote "Ben Hur" right there in the palace in Santa Fé. He was a brave man and he had to be, because governing around here was dangerous work. It meant killing or being killed.

8

BOZE. Attaboy, Mr. Maple. Tell 'em about the time you took a shot at Billy the Kid.

(JASON *hands* BOZE *Camels and change.*)

GRAMP. I didn't take no shots at the Kid. I had too God-damn much sense. But he took a couple at me. I'm practically the only man he ever missed; but he was only doing it in fun, so it couldn't hardly count.

(GABBY MAPLE *comes in from* L. *on the cue :"he ever missed." She is young and pretty, with a certain amount of style about her. Her principal distinguishing feature is an odd look of resentment in her large, dark eyes. She carries a thin book, her forefinger marking the place. She sits down at table at* L. *and starts to read.*)

JASON. Get on out with those Camels.

BOZE. O. K., boss. (*He goes out, with a knowing look at* GABBY *which she ignores.*)

1ST LINEMAN. Well, Pop, it's been very interesting, but I've got to be . . .

GRAMP. Wait a minute. I was just going to tell you about the first message we ever sent over that line. General Wallace dictated it and we sent it all the way through to Washington to President Hayes. And do you want to know what it said? It said, "God Save the Republic!" That's what General Wallace told us to say—and he was a great author.

1ST LINEMAN. (*Who has risen.*) You better send that same message through again, Pop—because the old republic's badly in need of assistance. How much do we owe? (*He has crossed to lunch counter, the* 2ND LINEMAN *following.*)

JASON. That'll be fifty-five cents apiece.

GABBY. What did they have?

JASON. Hamburger special, pie, and two cups of coffee.

GABBY. All right. (*She puts down book and picks up pie plates and coffee mugs and goes out into kitchen at* L. LINEMEN *are paying at counter.*)

GRAMP. Hope you'll call in again, boys. I always enjoy talking to anybody in the telegraphing business.

2ND LINEMAN. Maybe we will, Pop. Never can tell where we'll be sent next.

GRAMP. That's right—you can't.

9

JASON. (*As he shoves change across counter.*) There's just one remark I'd like to pass to you, brother. Just watch out how you talk about the United States of America.

1ST LINEMAN. What do you mean?

JASON. I mean simply this: belittling our system of government, preaching revolution and destruction, and red propaganda—well, it isn't a very healthy occupation. That's all.

GRAMP. I thought you said not to argue with the guests.

JASON. I'm only telling you, brother—for the sake of your own good.

1ST LINEMAN. So it's unhealthy, eh! How do you think this government was started if it wasn't by revolution?

2ND LINEMAN. Come on, Nick. We got to get going.

1ST LINEMAN. Wait till he answers my question.

JASON. The American Revolution was fought to establish law and order. But the object of your dirty red propaganda is to destroy it . . .

1ST LINEMAN. And how much law and order have *we* got? Did you read about that massacre yesterday in Oklahoma City? What kind of law and order is that?

2ND LINEMAN. Listen, Nick. I got a dame waiting up for me in Gallup and I . . .

JASON. If some of you Bolsheviks would quit preaching disrespect for law, it wouldn't be possible for criminals to . . .

1ST LINEMAN. Yeah? Do you want to know something? They don't have crime in Russia. And why? Because they've abolished the cause of crime. They've abolished greed! And I'll tell you something else . . .

2ND LINEMAN. I'm going. (*He starts out.*)

JASON. You got your eats and there's your change. Now kindly get out.

1ST LINEMAN. (*Pocketing his change.*) O. K., Mr. Tin-horn Patriot. I only hope I'm around here when it happens. I want to see you when you've joined the mob and started waving the red flag. (*He turns and starts out.*)

GRAMP. 'Bye, boys.

1ST LINEMAN. Good-bye, Pop. (LINEMEN *go out.*)

GRAMP. You never should get into arguments with a boy like that, Jason. You only make a fool out of yourself.

JASON. (*Back of counter.*) I'm sorry I didn't get his name, so's I could report him.

GRAMP. You tend to your own business, son, and stop fussing about other . . .

JASON. (*With surprising vehemence.*) My own business! That's a fine thing to say to me. What business have J got? Miserable little service station on the edge of nowheres.

GRAMP. It's a living, ain't it?

JASON. A living—yes—just barely. But it's one hell of a life for a man that ought to be getting some place in the world.

GRAMP. Maybe it's all you're good for.

JASON. I know—that's what *you* think. It's what you've always thought, since I was a boy. What chance have I ever had to prove what I can do?

GRAMP. You had a war, didn't you? Biggest war yet.

JASON. Yes—and you think I failed in that because I didn't come home with a lot of medals, and some German scalps hanging on my belt. Well, they didn't hand out medals to us soldiers that drove trucks—even if we did get right up into the danger zone time and time again.

GRAMP. All right, son—all right! You could have enlisted in the infantry if you'd had a mind to.

JASON. (*Hotly.*) I enlisted in the branch of the service where my knowledge of mechanics could do the most good to my country. And I've still got that knowledge. And you know damned well it's your fault I don't get more scope for using it. (*He has come out from behind counter.*)

GRAMP. My fault?

JASON. That's what I said. Hanging on to this place when you can sell it for good money.

GRAMP. I don't have to sell if I don't want to.

JASON. Dana Trimble's renewed his offer. Seven thousand dollars, and I know I can get him up to nine, maybe ten.

GRAMP. What makes him think this property's worth that much?

JASON. He knows perfectly well they're going to make this an interstate highway and run the bus route to El Paso through here.

GRAMP. All right—if it's good for him, it's good for us.

JASON. With seven thousand dollars I could buy a big piece of an Auto Camp on Redondo Boulevard in one of the best districts of

Los Angeles. I'd put in a Bar-B-Q service and in a couple of years we'd *have* something . . .

GRAMP. Los Angeles! My God! You want to go to Los Angeles and Gabby wants to go to Europe. Ain't they nobody around here that's satisfied to stay put?

JASON. How about yourself? Were you ever satisfied to stay put, until you got so damned old you didn't have enough energy to move?

GRAMP. Listen to me, son. In my day, we had places to go—*new* places. But, my God—Los Angeles . . . (GABBY *comes in from kitchen.*)

GABBY. Paula's scared.

GRAMP. What's she scared of?

GABBY. The Mexicans are saying that Mantee is headed this way.

JASON. He was headed for the border and he's over it by now—if the Texas Rangers haven't got him.

GRAMP. They won't get him. Have you seen his picture? Straight black hair. Got Injun blood. He'll fool 'em.

JASON. (*Importantly.*) You can't fool all the people all the time. (*He turns to go.*) Watch the counter, will you, Gabby? I got to get dressed.

GRAMP. Dressed? For what?

JASON. Legion meeting.

GABBY. What time will you be home, Dad?

JASON. About ten, I guess—maybe later. There's a lot of important business coming up. (*He addresses* GRAMP, *with some defiance.*) And I'm going to make some inquiries about those telegraph men. And if I can locate 'em, that Bolshevik will be out of a job and then he can go look for work pioneering in Russia.

GABBY. What'll you do—blow a bugle and turn the whole God-damn Legion loose on him?

JASON. Will you kindly control your language?

GABBY. I'll talk the only language I understand.

GRAMP. You'll never get Gabby to talk respectable. Never in all this world.

JASON. Well, I only hope some day my own daughter will learn to cultivate a little respect for the things I stand for. Maybe the time will come when you'll be thankful your father fought for his country. (*He goes out at* L.)

12

GABBY. (*Going behind counter.*) What did that telegraph man say that got Dad in such a stew?

GRAMP. I don't know what he said—something about Russia and pioneering. But there's a lot in it, whatever it was. The trouble with this country is, it's got settled. It's camped down in the bed of a dried-up river, and whenever anybody says, "Let's get the hell out of here," all the rest start to holler, "If we move a step the Injuns'll get us." Well—say—if we'd been that way in my time, I'd like to know how this country'd ever have got rich enough to be able to support the American Legion. (*Two toots from an auto horn are heard.*) Say! There's the mail. (*With surprising alacrity,* GRAMP *jumps up and hurries out.* GABBY *has poured herself a cup of coffee and brought it down to table at* L. *She sits down, sips coffee, opens her book, and reads. After a moment* BOZE *comes in, sees that she is alone, and closes door behind him.* GABBY *looks up, sees who it is, indicates indifference, and resumes reading.* BOZE *comes up behind her, leans over and kisses the back of her neck. She brushes him off as though he were a fly.*)

GABBY. (*Without vehemence.*) Cut it out. (BOZE *grins, draws up a chair, and sits down close to her, his hefty forearms resting on table.*)

BOZE. Not mad, are you, Gabby?

GABBY. Where's Gramp?

BOZE. He's out talking to the postman. Don't worry about him.

GABBY. I wasn't worrying.

BOZE. Don't you like me, honey sweet?

GABBY. No—not very much.

BOZE. O. K. I'll forgive you—seeing as I've been here only a little while and I haven't had much chance to go into my act. But when I do—you're going to change your attitude awful fast. (*She fails to comment on this threat. He is silent for a moment, his jaws confidently chewing on a small piece of gum.*) What's that you're reading?

GABBY. You wouldn't like it.

BOZE. How do *you* know how I feel about things? Can I look?

GABBY. Sure. Go ahead and look. (*He takes opened book and examines it.*)

BOZE. Hah—Poems. (*He reads.*)
> "The shapely slender shoulders small,
> Long arms, hands wrought in glorious wise,

13

Round little breasts, the hips withal
High, full of flesh, not scant of size,
Fit for all amorous masteries . . ."
(*He whistles through his teeth.*) Say! That's kind of pash! (*She snatches book away from him.*) So that's the kind of stuff you read. . . . Well, honey, I'm not a bit surprised. I've been suspecting all along that all you needed was a little encouragement. (*She looks at him, curiously, with a mixture of contempt and some slight interest.*) And I don't wonder that in a God-forsaken place like this you'd have to get it out of poetry.

GABBY. (*Defensive.*) It's great poetry!

BOZE. Certainly it's great. But I can think of something a whole lot better. . . . Look at me, honey. (*She looks at him.*) I'm not so terrible looking, am I?

GABBY. Why do you wear that locket around your neck?

BOZE. (*Laughing.*) Locket!

GABBY. It makes you look like a sissy.

BOZE. I've been waiting for you to notice that. That was my father's watch chain. My mother gave it to me when I graduated. I'd like you to know my mother. She lives in Grants Pass, Oregon, and she could tell you some pretty nice things about me. But wait till you see what's on the end. (*He draws chain out and displays a gold football.*) It's a gold football—solid gold! I got that for intercepting a pass and running sixty-eight yards for a touchdown.

GABBY. What was your school?

BOZE. Nevada Tech. If I'd been with Princeton or Minnesota or any of those big clubs, I'd have been All-American. Wait till I show you something. (*He produces a billfold from his hip pocket and extracts therefrom a frequently folded clipping.*) That's from Sid Ziff's column in the *Los Angeles Herald*. He saw me play against Loyola. Listen to what he says: "Tip to the pigskin fraternity: When pondering your All-American selections for this current Anno Domini, just mull over the name of Boze Hertzlinger of Nevada Tech. Playing with an admittedly minor league club, and protected by interference of cellophane strength, Hertzlinger managed to remind some of us observers of the Illini Phantom himself." Do you know who the Illini Phantom was? Red Grange! (*He folds up clipping and restores it to his pocket.*) That's just a sample of the kind of notices I got. I could show you dozens more like it.

14

GABBY. You think a hell of a lot of yourself, don't you?

BOZE. (Disarmingly.) Who wouldn't, in my position?

GABBY. Why do you have to work in a filling station?

BOZE. Well—that's a point that I don't know if I could explain so's you'd understand it. I could be making good money in a lot of ways right now—engineering, coaching, the insurance game—lots of ways. But—I just can't be tied down—not yet. I've got an itch inside here that keeps me on the move—chasing the rainbow.

GABBY. Do you ever expect to catch it?

BOZE. I'll catch it all right. I'll twist its tail, and make it do tricks. . . . Maybe I'm kind of close to it right now.

GABBY. You'd better look some place else. There aren't any rainbows around Black Mesa.

BOZE. I wouldn't bet on that. . . . You know, Gabby—you're a queer kid. Sometimes you seem too young to know anything. And then—sometimes—you seem like God's grandmother. And reading that pash poetry. That gives me an idea.

GABBY. An idea of what?

BOZE. Oh—it's easy to tell when a girl's ready for love.

GABBY. How do you tell that, Boze?

BOZE. Well—one pretty sure way is when she starts calling me by my own name for the first time. And another way is how I feel myself. It takes two to make a radio program, you know—the one that's sending, and the one that's receiving. And when I'm with a girl that's cute and appealing, with big, soft eyes—well—I can feel sort of electric waves running all through me—and I can be pretty sure she's doing some broadcasting, whether she knows it or not.

GABBY. Have you got a program coming in now?

BOZE. Listen —— It's like the hottest torch song that ever was sung. Can't you kind of hear it, honey? (She looks away from him, but says nothing. He reaches out and takes hold of her hand, entwining his fingers with hers.) You can call me a sap if you want to, Gabby—but I guess I'm falling in love with you. I'm getting so I want you more than is good for me.

GABBY. (Looking at him, levelly.) Have you ever been in love before?

BOZE. (Scornfully.) No!

GABBY. Have you ever said you were?

BOZE. Sure—plenty of times.

15

GABBY. Did they believe you?

BOZE. (*Amused.*) Certainly they did. And I'll tell you why: it's because they were all dumb! But that's just where you're different. I couldn't fool you, Gabby.

GABBY. I'm smart, am I?

BOZE. Too smart—for most men. You'd catch on to 'em. But that's what I want. Because the more you see into me, the better you're going to like me. (*With his free hand, he takes hold of her chin.*)

GABBY. You'd better look out, if you want to hold on to your job. Dad might come in and he doesn't like to have the help making passes at me.

BOZE. That wouldn't bother me, honey sweet. There are plenty more jobs for anyone with the ambition I've got. But there aren't plenty more girls like you. (*He leans over and kisses her.*) You're going to love me, Gabby. You're going to love me a lot.

GABBY. Look out! There's someone . . .

BOZE. (*Unconcerned.*) We'll talk about it some more later.

(ALAN SQUIER *has appeared in doorway, and, seeing that he has interrupted some amour, has paused to give them time to break. He is a thin, wan, vague man of about thirty-five. He wears a brown felt hat, brown tweed coat and gray flannel trousers—which came originally but much too long ago from the best Saville Row tailors. He is shabby and dusty but there is about him a sort of afterglow of elegance. There is something about him—and it is impossible in a stage direction to say just what it is—that brings to mind the ugly word "condemned." He carries a heavy walking stick and a rucksack is slung over his shoulders. He is diffident in manner, ultra-polite and soft spoken, his accent is that of an Anglicized American.*)

SQUIER. Good evening.

BOZE. (*Cordially.*) Good evening! What can we do for you?

SQUIER. Can I order something to eat?

BOZE. Why, certainly. Miss Maple will take care of you. (*While* SQUIER *is taking off his rucksack and hat, and putting them on bench at* R., BOZE *turns to* GABBY *and speaks in a low tone.*) Your father going into town?

GABBY. Yes. (*She is taking a menu card to table at* C.)

BOZE. (*Significantly.*) O. K. (*He goes out.*)

GABBY. Will you sit down here, sir?

SQUIER. Thanks. (*He sits. She hands him menu card.*)

16

GABBY. Driven far?

SQUIER. I've been walking.

GABBY. Do you live around here?

SQUIER. No. My last host of the road reached his own ranch, about ten miles back, and didn't ask me in. I had to continue on foot. It's wonderful what progress you can make just by doing this. (*He jerks his thumb and looks at menu.*) "Today's Special." . . . Just what is a Bar-B-Q?

GABBY. Well—here it's hamburger sandwich with vegetables on the side. It's always "Today's Special." But it's pretty good.

SQUIER. I want it. But first I'd like some of that cream of corn soup, and some beer, and—I'll order the dessert later.

GABBY. O. K. (*She takes menu.*)

SQUIER. Another question. Where am I?

GABBY. This place is called Black Mesa, but there's nothing else here. Where were you planning to go?

SQUIER. My plans have been uncertain.

GABBY. You mean, you were just bumming along?

SQUIER. Call it gipsying. I had a vague idea that I'd like to see the Pacific Ocean, and perhaps drown in it. But that depends . . .

GABBY. Where did you come from?

SQUIER. Quite a long way, Miss Maple. Is that the name?

GABBY. (*Smiling.*) Yes—that's it. Are you English?

SQUIER. No. You might call me an American once removed. . . . But—if you don't mind ——

GABBY. The soup'll be right in. The washroom's through there, on your left, if you want it. (*She indicates door at L.*)

SQUIER. Thank you. (GABBY *goes out at* L. SQUIER *rises. He sees book of verse, picks it up and looks at it, wonderingly. The door at* L. *opens and* JASON *comes out, resplendent in the uniform of his Legion post. It is horizon blue, with white Sam Browne belt and pistol holster.* SQUIER *looks at* JASON *with amazement.*)

JASON. Good evening.

SQUIER. Good evening.

JASON. Anyone take your order?

SQUIER. Yes—a charming young lady. . . .

JASON. That's my daughter. (*He says this with a note of warning, as much as to add: "And don't try to get fresh."* JASON *crosses to cash register, punches the "No Sale," and extracts five silver dollars from till. He then reaches under counter, takes out*

17

a revolver, breaks it to make sure it's loaded, and rubs it with a cloth. SQUIER has one more puzzled look at him, then goes out at L. GRAMP comes in from upper R., bearing a fresh copy of the Denver Post.)

GRAMP. (At end of counter.) I was just talking to Roy Greeley and he says in town they're all certain that Mantee outfit is headed here. Look! They got the whole story here in The Post. Oklahoma City Massacre! Six killed—four wounded—two not expected to live. (JASON glances at paper.) The sheriff's got all his deputies out patrolling the roads. They think there's sure going to be some killing around here.

JASON. Well—if there is—we can't trust that sheriff to do a damn thing. We'll turn out the Legion.

GRAMP. You would?

JASON. Certainly! That's what we're there for. (He thrusts revolver in holster of his Sam Browne belt, goes to kitchen door, and calls through it: "Gabby!")

GABBY'S VOICE. Yes?

JASON. I'm leaving now. And I—I took five bucks. If anything delays me getting back, I'll phone.

GABBY'S VOICE. O. K.

JASON. Don't forget to light the Neon sign when it gets dark.

GABBY'S VOICE. I won't. (He shuts kitchen door and crosses up front of counter.)

GRAMP. Well, by God, you'd better not try to do any shooting in that get-up. I never seed a better target.

JASON. You needn't be afraid about me. (GABBY comes in with soup.)

GRAMP. I ain't afraid. But I would be if I was you.

GABBY. How much did you say you took?

JASON. Five bucks.

GABBY. What do you need all that for?

JASON. Just in case of emergency. (He decides to resent all this interference.) By God, between the two of you, you'd think I wasn't fit to be trusted with money or ideas or anything. But I'm here to tell you, both of you . . .

GABBY. (Putting soup on table.) What, Dad?

JASON. Oh, never mind. (He goes out. GABBY goes to counter, opens a bottle of beer, and takes it to C. table.)

GRAMP. (While she is about this.) It's too bad they didn't wear a

18

uniform like that when they fit the Germans. They wouldn't none of 'em have come home. . . . Who's that food for?

GABBY. Customer. He's in the washroom, I guess.

GRAMP. Is it that young feller that walked in with a little pack on his back? (*He goes to his rocking chair at* L.)

GABBY. Yes—that's the one.

GRAMP. Looked to me like one of them things you see up around Taos. (*He sits down.*) Hey, Gabby, how about letting your poor, weary old grandfather have a little drink now?

GABBY. No.

GRAMP. Aw—come on. I ain't got so long to live. (SQUIER *comes in from* L.)

GABBY. You can have one before you go to bed, and that's all.

(*She goes out through kitchen door.*)

GRAMP. Your soup's waiting for you, my friend.

SQUIER. Thank you.

GRAMP. Looks good, too.

SQUIER. Yes. It looks fine. (SQUIER *sit downs and starts to eat, ravenously.* GRAMP *decides that the Denver Post will serve as a conversation opener. He crosses to* SQUIER'S *table.*)

GRAMP. Like to see a picture of that Duke Mantee? (*He holds out newspaper.* SQUIER *looks at clamorous headlines.*)

SQUIER. My God! Six killed. Did he do all that?

GRAMP. Him and his friends did, when they sprung him from the law. Fine lot of sheriffs they must have there in Oklahoma City— letting themselves get knocked over right out in front of the Court House

SQUIER. (*Still eating.*) He doesn't look very vicious, does he?

GRAMP. (*Sitting down.*) Well—I'll tell you; you can't tell a killer from his picture, except by his chin. That's a funny thing about a killer—always holds his chin in. Ever notice that?

SQUIER. (*Buttering some bread.*) I don't think I've ever seen a killer.

GRAMP. I have. Plenty of 'em. Ever hear of Billy the Kid?

SQUIER. Yes, indeed.

GRAMP. I knowed him well, down in the Pecos country. (*Proudly.*) He took a couple of shots at me, once.

SQUIER. I congratulate you on still being with us.

GRAMP. Well—it was kind of dark, and he'd had a few—and,

19

besides, I don't think he really meant to do me any real harm. Just wanted to scare the pants off of me.

SQUIER. Did he do it?

GRAMP. Naw—I seed he was just having some fun. So I said to him: "Kid—you're drunk!" And he said, "What makes you think that?" He was always soft-spoken. And I said: "Because you missed me!" Well, sir—he had to laugh. . . . You're kind of hongry, aren't you?

SQUIER. Yes. You can go just so long without food . . .

GRAMP. Been having some bad luck?

SQUIER. Yes.

GRAMP. Well—no disgrace in that these days. What line of work you in?

SQUIER. None, just now. I have been, at times, a writer.

GRAMP. A writer, eh? That's a funny thing. . . .

SQUIER. (Laughing silently.) Yes—it is.

GRAMP. I knew the greatest writer that ever lived. Sam Clemens. Ever hear of him?

SQUIER. (Trying hard to think.) Let me see . . .

GRAMP. Well, did you ever hear of Mark Twain?

SQUIER. Oh, yes!

GRAMP. Same feller!

SQUIER. Really? (GABBY comes in with "Today's Special," which she puts on table.)

GRAMP. Yes, sir. I knew him when I was a boy up in Virginia City. He was writing comical pieces for the paper there—The Enterprise—and he was the best God-damn liar I ever seed, and I've seed plenty. He used to say he did his writing on the principle that his readers wanted everything but the truth, so that's what he give 'em. (GABBY is on the way out.) Are you a famous writer? (At kitchen door, GABBY turns to look at SQUIER, then goes out.)

SQUIER. No.

GRAMP. Maybe you're just modest. What's your name?

SQUIER. Alan Squier.

GRAMP. Well, maybe you are famous, for all I'd know. I don't get to do much reading, outside of the headlines. Eyes have gone back on me. But when I was your age, I could hit a running jack rabbit at fifty paces . . .

GABBY. (Coming in.) Your supper's ready, Gramp

20

GRAMP. And I'm ready for it. Got *me* hongry, watching him eat. (*He has risen.*) Pleased to have met you, Mr. Squier.

SQUIER. Pleased to have met *you*, sir.

GRAMP. Yes, sir. Thank you, sir. (*He goes out.*)

GABBY. Like the soup?

SQUIER. (*From the heart.*) It was glorious!

GABBY. Want some coffee?

SQUIER. Will it mix with the beer?

GABBY. Oh, sure. Coffee will mix with anything. (*She goes to counter to get his coffee.*)

SQUIER. That's a charming old gentleman. Your grandfather?

GABBY. Yes.

SQUIER. He told me he'd been missed by Billy the Kid.

GABBY. He tells everybody about that. Poor Gramp. You get terribly sick of him after a while. (*She has brought down coffee.*) Did I hear him say you're a writer?

SQUIER. (*Humbly.*) Yes.

GABBY. I haven't met many writers—except Sidney Wenzell. Ever heard of him?

SQUIER. That's not Mark Twain, is it?

GABBY. No! Sidney Wenzell—he's with Warner Brothers. He stopped here once, when he was driving out to the Coast. He said I ought to go to Hollywood, and to be sure and look him up. But—what the hell! They never mean it.

SQUIER. No! They never mean a thing. (*She has picked up her book and started to go.*) Please don't go. (*She pauses and turns.*)

GABBY. Something else you want? We got pie and layer cake.

SQUIER. No. I—I'd like to talk to you. Please sit down.

GABBY. All right. (*She sits down, across from him, at C. table.* SQUIER *eats rapidly, mechanically, during the subsequent dialogue, stowing food away as he talks and listens.*)

SQUIER. I suppose you want to go into the movies?

GABBY. (*Scornfully.*) God, *no!*

SQUIER. But—I thought every beautiful girl had her heart set on Hollywood.

GABBY. That's just it. It's too common. I want to go to Bourges.

(*She fails to soften the "G."*)

SQUIER. Where?

GABBY. Bourges—in France. You'd never guess it, but that's where I came from.

SQUIER. You're not French?

GABBY. Partly. I was born in Bourges—but I left it almost before I was able to walk, so all I know about it is from the picture postcards my mother sends me. They got a cathedral there.

SQUIER. Your mother still lives there?

GABBY. Yes. Dad brought us back here after the war. Mother stuck it out in this desert for a couple of years, and then she packed up and went back to Bourges. We've never seen her since. Some people seem to think it was cruel of her to leave me. But what could she do? She didn't have any money to bring me up. She just couldn't *live* here—and you can't blame her for that. Do you think she was cruel?

SQUIER. Not if you don't, Miss Maple.

GABBY. Well—I *don't*. She's tried lots of times to get me over there to see her—but Dad won't allow it. She got a divorce and married a Frenchman that's got a bookstore. Mother was always a great reader, so I guess it's nice for her. She's got three more kids. Just think of that! I've got a half-brother and half-sisters that can't speak a word of English. I'd sure like to see them.

SQUIER. Can you speak French?

GABBY. Only what you learn in high school—like *table* for "table." (*She takes photograph from book.*) Look—there's my mother's picture. That was just before she married Dad. She had her picture taken smelling a rose.

SQUIER. She's lovely! And I can see the resemblance.

GABBY. It's hard to imagine her being married to Dad, isn't it? But I guess he looked all right in his American uniform. Mother used to send me a book every year for my birthday, but they were all in French and I couldn't read them. So last year I wrote and asked if she'd mind sending me one in English, and she sent me this one. It's the Poems of François Villon. Ever read it?

SQUIER. Yes.

GABBY. It's wonderful poetry. She wrote in it: "*à ma chère petite Gabrielle.*" That means "to my dear little Gabrielle." She gave me that name. It's about the only French thing I've got.

SQUIER. Gabrielle. It's a beautiful name.

GABBY. Wouldn't you know it would get changed into "Gabby"

22

by these ignorant bastards around here? I guess you think I use terrible language.

SQUIER. Oh, no! It—it's picturesque.

GABBY. Well—it suits this kind of country.

SQUIER. You share your mother's opinion of the desert? (*She nods.*) But you can find solace in the Poems of François Villon.

GABBY. Yes. They get the stink of the gasoline and the hamburger out of my system.

SQUIER. Would you like to read me one of those poems, Gabrielle?

GABBY. You mean now?

SQUIER. Yes. While I'm finishing "Today's Special."

GABBY. O. K. I'll read you the one I like best. He wrote it about a friend of his who was getting married. (*She reads, with marked but inexpert emphasis:*)

> "At daybreak, when the falcon claps his wings
> No whit for grief, but noble heart held high
> With loud glad noise he stirs himself and springs,
> And takes his meat and toward his lure draws nigh;
> Such good I wish you! Yea, and heartily
> I'm fired with hope of true love's meed to get;
> Knowing Love writes it in his book; for why,
> This is the end for which we twain are met."

Did you ever see a falcon?

SQUIER. Yes.

GABBY. What does it look like?

SQUIER. Not very pleasant. Like a hawk. Go on, Gabrielle.

GABBY. (*Resuming reading.*)

> "Mine own heart's lady with no gain-sayings
> You shall be always till I die;
> And in my right against all bitter things
> Sweet laurel with fresh rose its force shall try;
> Seeing reason wills not that I cast love by
> Nor here with reason shall I chide and fret

(*She closes book and recites:*)

> Nor cease to serve, but serve more constantly;
> This is the end for which we twain are met."

(*She looks at him, and he at her. Then he resumes his attack on hamburger.*) You know—that's wonderful stuff. But that's the way the French people are: they can understand everything—like life,

23

and love—and death—and they can enjoy it, or laugh at it, depending on how they feel.

SQUIER. And that's why you want to go to France—for understanding.

GABBY. I *will* go there! When Gramp dies, we can sell this place. Dad's going to take his share and move to Los Angeles, so that he can join a really big Legion post and get to be a political power. But I'm going to spend my part of the money on a trip to Bourges, where there's something beautiful to look at, and wine, and dancing in the streets.

SQUIER. If I were you—I'd stay here, Gabrielle, and avoid disappointment.

GABBY. What makes you think I'd be disappointed?

SQUIER. I've been to France.

GABBY. You were there in the war?

SQUIER. No, I missed that. But I lived there for eight years, through seventeen changes of government.

GABBY. What were you doing—writing books?

SQUIER. No—planning to write books. You know what a gigolo is?

GABBY. Were *you* one of those? (*He nods.*) You danced with women for money?

SQUIER. Oh lord, no! I never was a good enough dancer for that. I—I married.

GABBY. Oh.

SQUIER. Please don't think too ill of me. I once actually wrote a book.

GABBY. What was it—fiction?

SQUIER. In a sense. It was a novel about the bleak, glacier-stripped hills of my native New England. I was twenty-two when I wrote it, and it was very, very stark. It sold slightly over six hundred copies. It cost the publisher quite a lot of money, and it also cost him his wife. You see, she divorced him and married me. She had faith in me, and she had the chance to display it, because her husband was very generous in the financial settlement. I suppose he had faith in me, too. She saw in me a major artist, profound, but inarticulate. She believed that all I needed was background, and she gave it to me—with southern exposure and a fine view of the Mediterranean. That was considered the thing to do in the period that followed Scott Fitzgerald. For eight years I reclined there, on the Riviera, on my background—and I waited for the major artist to step forth and say something of enduring importance. He preferred to remain inarticulate.

GABBY. And you've left your wife, now?

SQUIER. Yes.

GABBY. I'm glad you did.

SQUIER. I left her at her suggestion. She has taken up with a Brazilian painter—also a major artist. There was nothing for me to do but travel. I decided to go forth and discover America—and I've gone this far on my journey, thanks to the power of the thumb. (*He gestures with his thumb.*)

GABBY. What were you looking for?

SQUIER. Well—that's rather hard to say. I—I suppose I've been looking for something to believe in. I've been hoping to find something that's worth living for—and dying for.

GABBY. What have you found?

SQUIER. Nothing so interesting as an old man who was missed by Billy the Kid, and a fair young lady who reads Villon.

GABBY. (*After a pause.*) Well—I do other things that'd surprise you.

SQUIER. I'm sure you do.

GABBY. I wouldn't tell this to everybody—but you—well, you're kind of . . .

SQUIER. I'm kind of nobody. What is it, Gabrielle?

GABBY. I paint pictures.

SQUIER. Are they any good?

GABBY. Hell, no!

SQUIER. Could I see them?

GABBY. Oh—I never let people look at them. I'd only get kidded. They're kind of crazy pictures.

SQUIER. All the better. Please let me see them.

GABBY. You know anything about art?

SQUIER. Oh—I've studied the whole cycle—right from El Greco through Burne Jones and back to El Greco again. Perhaps you're another genius. Perhaps it's my mission to introduce you to posterity.

GABBY. Are you kidding me?

SQUIER. No, Gabrielle. I've never kidded anybody outside of myself. (*The voice of* HERB, *a cowboy, is heard offstage.*)

GABBY. All right. But you've got to promise not to tell anybody.

SQUIER. My word of honor—for all it's worth. (GABBY *goes out.*)

25

HERB'S VOICE. Sure, Boze. I know you've got all the inside dope. But I'll bet you four bits he flattens him inside of five rounds.

BOZE. Four bits to what?

HERB. No—I ain't giving you no odds.

BOZE. All right!

HERB. All right! (HERB *has come in during this cheerful chal-lenge. He wears a big black hat, gray shirt and blue overalls, and carries a gunny sack. Genially, to* SQUIER.) How de do.

SQUIER. (*Still eating.*) Good evening.

HERB. Where's Gab?

SQUIER. She'll be back in a moment. (HERB *has crossed to counter.*)

HERB. They sure give you a good meal here, don't they?

SQUIER. Superb!

HERB. Well—I'll tell you. Jason Maple's got a natural-born gift for hotel keeping, and by God I think Gabby's better at it than he is. The only trouble with 'em is, they ain't got a hotel. (*He has to laugh at that.*)

SQUIER. Yes—that does restrict the full play of their talents. (GABBY *comes in with a sheaf of water color paintings of compara-tively small size but of virulent color.*)

HERB. Hi, Gab.

GABBY. Hi, Herb. (*Nervously she puts pictures face down on table by* SQUIER. *She cautions him with a look not to display them to* HERB. *But during subsequent dialogue,* SQUIER *peeks at them with a certain amount of neck-stroking bewilderment.*)

HERB. Got any moon?

GABBY. Sure.

HERB. How much you asking for it?

GABBY. A dollar fifty a bottle.

HERB. Holy Cow! Well—give us a bottle, and half a dozen bottles of beer.

GABBY. You fellers going to get drunk tonight? (*She has gone to counter to fill order.*)

HERB. (*Leaning on counter.*) By God—that's the way it looks. Sheriff called up the old man and asked if we could be spared for patrolling the roads and the old man says sure and the sheriff says he'll come out and swear us in, but he ain't come yet, so we got a poker game started up the road a piece and thought we might as well have something to go along with it.

GABBY. There you are, Herb. That'll be two thirty.

HERB. All I got's two bucks. (*He tenders it.*) Will you trust me for the thirty cents?

GABBY. I'll take back two bottles of beer. That'll make it even.

HERB. (*As he dumps bottles into gunnysack.*) Gosh—liquor sure is getting expensive these days. Well—I guess we got enough here seeing as there's only three of us.

GABBY. How you going to play poker if you haven't got any more money?

HERB. Oh, we got a book. So long, Gabby.

GABBY. So long, Herb. (*He goes out.* GABBY *rings up the two dollars in cash register and comes down. She is eager to know how* SQUIER *feels about her paintings, but she is trying desperately hard to be offhand about it.*) They're terrible, aren't they? (SQUIER *is now examining pictures with rapt attention.*)

SQUIER. I—I don't know. Is—this a portrait of someone?

GABBY. That's Paula, our Mexican cook. She's the only one knows I ever try to do that junk. It isn't much of a likeness.

SQUIER. I'm sure it wasn't intended to be. (*He picks up another picture.*) Certainly no critic could condemn you for being photographic.

GABBY. This is the one I like best. (SQUIER *looks at it.*) I wanted to show how the storm clouds look when they roll down from the mountains.

SQUIER. What made you paint in this strange manner?

GABBY. It's—just the way I feel.

SQUIER. You're a product of the ultimate French school, all right.

GABBY. (*Pleased.*) You think so?

SQUIER. These are somewhat in the Dufy manner—and yet—a lot less conventional.

GABBY. But are they any *good*?

SQUIER. I tell you, Gabrielle—I can't say. I'm tremendously impressed and, also, bewildered.

GABBY. I'll bet I could improve if I could get to France. You know, they've got some of the finest art schools in the world there. And they've got beautiful things to paint, too—flowers, and castles and rivers. But here in this desert—it's just the same thing over and over again.

SQUIER. Don't you realize—there are probably thousands of artists in France today who are saying, "I'd find a really big theme

27

for my canvas if I could only get out to Arizona."

GABBY. I know. A lot of people come out here and go crazy about the desert. They say it's full of mystery, and it's haunted, and all that. Well—maybe it is. But there's something in me that makes me want something different.

SQUIER. (Looking at her.) I know there's something in you. I wish I could figure out what it is.

GABBY. Listen—you've been in France. What are they like there?

SQUIER. Well—it's rather difficult to render a sweeping judgment.

GABBY. I've always imagined they must all be like Villon—gay, reckless, poetic.

SQUIER. No—I shouldn't call them any of those things. Especially, not reckless!

GABBY. But they're always having a good time, aren't they?

SQUIER. Not invariably.

GABBY. Maybe I know them better than you do, because it's in my blood. Sometimes I can feel as though I were sparkling all over, and I don't care what happens—I want to go out and do something that's absolutely crazy—and marvelous. But then the American part of me speaks up and spoils everything. It makes me go to work and figure out a lot of dull accounts; so many pounds of coffee, so many frankf·· ·ers, so many rolls. . . .

SQUIER. You keep the accounts correctly?

GABBY. If I didn't, this place would be bankrupt.

SQUIER. Then that's the French part of you. The sparkle must be one hundred per cent American. Would you like to marry a Frenchman?

GABBY. I don't want to marry anybody. I want to always be free!

SQUIER. How about that stalwart youth out there in the football jersey?

GABBY. What makes you think I'd take any notice of him?

SQUIER. Well—when I came in here . . .

GABBY. Oh, sure. He was kissing me. That's nothing.

SQUIER. Perhaps. But there's always the chance of development.

GABBY. He's trying to make me. That's all he wants.

SQUIER. Do you think he'll succeed?

GABBY. I haven't decided yet. It would be experience, and that's what I need. Do you think I ought to give in?

SQUIER. Don't ask me, Gabrielle. Let your French blood guide you. It's infallible, in matters like that.

GABBY. But you ought to know *something*. You've seen a lot, and you've written a book, and you've been married . . .

SQUIER. I don't know anything. You see—the trouble with me is, I belong to a vanishing race. I'm one of the intellectuals.

GABBY. That means you've got brains. I can see you have.

SQUIER. Yes—brains without purpose. Noise without sound. Shape without substance. Have you ever read "The Hollow Men"? (*She shakes her head.*) Don't. It's discouraging, because it's true. It refers to the intellectuals, who thought they'd conquered Nature. They dammed it up, and used its waters to irrigate the waste-lands. They built streamlined monstrosities to penetrate its resistance. They wrapped it up in cellophane and sold it to drugstores. They were so certain they had it subdued. And now—do you realize what it is that is causing world chaos?

GABBY. No.

SQUIER. Well, I'm probably the only living person who can tell you. . . . It's Nature hitting back. Not with the old weapons—floods, plagues, holocausts. We can neutralize them. She's fighting back with strange instruments called neuroses. She's deliber-ately afflicting mankind with the jitters. Nature is proving that she can't be beaten—not by the likes of us. She's taking the world away from the intellectuals and giving it back to the apes. . . . Forgive me, Gabrielle . . . I can't tell you what a luxury it is to have some one to talk to. . . . But don't listen to me. I was born in 1901, the year Victoria died. I was just too late for the Great War—and too soon for the revolution. You're a war baby. You may be an entirely different species, for all I know. You can easily be one of Nature's own children, and therefore able to understand her, and laugh at her—or enjoy her—depend-ing on how you feel. You're the only one who can say whether or not you should yield to the ardors of Number 42 out there. (*He finishes his glass of beer.*) That beer is excellent.

GABBY. It's made in Phoenix. (*She is looking at him intently.*) You know—you talk like a God-damn fool.

SQUIER. I know it. (*He is taking out last of his cigarettes.*)

GABBY. No wonder your wife kicked you out. . . . And no won-der she fell for you in the first place. (*He pauses in act of light-ing his cigarette.*)

SQUIRE. That sounds alarmingly like a compliment.

GABBY. It is a compliment. What did you say your name was?

SQUIER. Alan Squier. I've been calling you Gabrielle, so you'd better . . .

GABBY. Where are you going from here, Alan?

SQUIER. That depends on where this road leads.

GABBY. It leads to the petrified forest.

SQUIER. What's that?

GABBY. Oh—just a lot of dead old trees in the desert, that have turned to stone.

SQUIER. The petrified forest! A suitable haven for me. Perhaps that's what I'm destined for—to make an interesting fossil for future study. Homo Semi-Americanus—a specimen of the in-between age.

GABBY. I was just thinking—I'd like to go to France with you. (He looks at her, sharply—then looks sharply away.)

SQUIER. Oh, no, Gabrielle! I could never retrace my footsteps.

GABBY. You mean you haven't enough money?

SQUIER. Even that is an understatement.

GABBY. I haven't enough, either—yet. But I can do this as well as you can. (She gestures with her thumb.)

SQUIER. We'd reach a point, on the Atlantic Coast, where even that gesture would be unavailing.

GABBY. You know, Alan—there's something about you that's very appealing.

SQUIER. Appealing! Yes—that's been my downfall. It was that very quality which led me into the gigolo trade.

GABBY. Why wouldn't you like to be a gigolo for me?

SQUIER. For one very good reason: you couldn't afford it.

GABBY. But I will be able to afford it.

SQUIER. On your share of this property? (He shakes his head.)

GABBY. Listen—I've got more than that coming to me. Do you know how much Gramp has got salted away in the bank in Santa Fé? Twenty-two thousand dollars! He had every cent of it in gold and silver in the safety vaults. Why—we didn't even know about it until the government passed a law against hoarding and they printed his name in the papers. It's in Liberty Bonds now, and it's all willed to me. I guess we could travel pretty far on that, couldn't we?

SQUIER. Too far.

GABBY. We could go to France, and you'd show me everything, all the cathedrals and the art—and explain everything. And you wouldn't have to marry me, Alan. We'd just live in sin and have one hell of a time.

SQUIER. That's a startling proposal, Gabrielle. I hadn't expected to receive anything like that in *this* desert.

GABBY. We'd have to wait—maybe years. But I could have Boze fired and give you the job tending the gas station.

SQUIER. You think you'd like to have me for a companion?

GABBY. I know I would. And I don't make mistakes. You're no ape-man, Alan—but you're lovable.

SQUIER. Lovable! The next grade below appealing.

GABBY. Wouldn't you like to be loved by me?

SQUIER. (*Looking at her intently.*) Yes, Gabrielle . . . I should like to be loved by you.

GABBY. You think I'm attractive?

SQUIER. There are better words than that for what you are.

GABBY. Then why don't we at least make a start at it? You haven't got anything else to do.

SQUIER. (*Smiling.*) No—that's just it. You couldn't live very long with a man who had nothing else to do but worship you. That's a dull kind of love, Gabrielle. It's the kind of love that makes people old, too soon. (*He rises.*) But—I thank you for the suggestion. You've opened up a new channel of my imagination which will be pleasant to explore during my lonely wanderings. I'll think of the chimes of Bourges—and you—and sin.

GABBY. You're going now?

SQUIER. Yes. And I shall continue going until either I drop or that major artist emerges to announce his message to posterity.

GABBY. (*Rising.*) Well—I can't stop you.

SQUIER. No, Gabrielle, you can't. But you can do me one great favor, before I go. . . . Would you mind very much if I kissed you good-bye? (GABBY *looks at him levelly.*)

GABBY. No. I wouldn't mind.

SQUIER. You'd understand that it would be nothing more . . .

GABBY. I'd understand. It'd be just a kiss—that's all.

SQUIER. That's absolutely all. (*He kisses her.* BOZE *is seen through glass of doorway. He bursts door open.*)

BOZE. Ah-hah! So that's what's been going on in here! Necking, huh! (*He strides up to* SQUIER *and seizes him by shoulder.*) Who the hell are you?

GABBY. Lay off him, Boze. (*She has seized her paintings.*)

31

BOZE. Just because she's cute and sweet you thought you could get fresh, huh!

GABBY. He didn't get fresh! He only wanted to kiss me good-bye.

SQUIER. Yes—the impulse is rather hard to explain—but I . . .

BOZE. You needn't wait to explain it. Pay your check and get out.

SQUIER. Very well. How much do I owe, Miss Maple?

GABBY. Thirty cents.

BOZE. Is that all he ate? (*He looks down at table at remains of* SQUIER'S *meal.*)

GABBY. Yes! Shut up!

SQUIER. Thirty cents, eh. Very reasonable. Very reasonable indeed! But—that brings us to another embarrassment. I—I haven't got thirty cents. I haven't anything.

BOZE. Well—by God—I didn't expect to find such nerve in anybody that looked like you. What are you going to do about it?

SQUIER. I haven't the remotest . . .

BOZE. What have you got in your pack there?

SQUIER. Shirt, underwear, socks, toothbrush, passport, an insurance policy, and a copy of Modern Man in Search of a Soul, by Dr. Jung.

BOZE. You thought you could pay with a kiss, did you? (*He seizes* SQUIER *again. A car is heard stopping.*) Thought if you brought a little romance into her poor, starved life the check'd be forgotten, did you?

GABBY. Take your hands off him, Boze. Go on, Alan, beat it!

SQUIER. I'll go.

BOZE. I'll just give you a little head start. (*He has* SQUIER *by the collar and is about to propel him out door, when* MR. *and* MRS. CHISHOLM *come in.* MR. CHISHOLM *is about forty-five—thin, dry, sharp, persnickety, with pince-nez eyeglasses.* MRS. CHISHOLM *is about ten years younger—rather attractive, rather chic, very world-weary. The* CHISHOLMS *belong to the topmost layer of society in Dayton, Ohio.*)

MRS. CHISHOLM. (*In an undertone to* GABBY.) Where is the Ladies' Room, please?

GABBY. This way, madam. (*She directs* MRS. CHISHOLM *to door at* L. *and points off.*) That door there, on your left.

MRS. CHISHOLM. Thank you. (JOSEPH, *the* CHISHOLMS' *Negro chauffeur, appears in doorway. He is short, elegant, wears a neat uniform and yellow glasses.*)

JOSEPH. We want fifteen gallons and a quart of oil.

BOZE. Be right with you. (*In an undertone to* SQUIER.) You ready to leave?

SQUIER. Just a moment—my rucksack.

GABBY. Get on the job, Boze. (*She goes up to lunch counter and hides her paintings.* BOZE *mutters something unpleasant to* SQUIER *and goes out.* SQUIER *is putting on his rucksack.*)

CHISHOLM. What kind of cigars have you?

GABBY. Admiration, White Owl, and Texas Dandies.

CHISHOLM. How much are the Texas Dandies?

GABBY. Three for a dime.

CHISHOLM. Let me have an Admiration.

GABBY. (*Offering him box.*) Come far?

CHISHOLM. (*Selecting one.*) Yes. We've driven from Dayton, Ohio. We're on our way out to Santa Barbara for the winter. (*As he pays for cigar.*) We lost a great deal of time today as I wanted Mrs. Chisholm to see the Gila cliff dwellings. She was rather disappointed. How far is it to the Phoenix Biltmore?

GABBY. It's a good two hundred miles from here. (*She hands him his change.*)

CHISHOLM. (*Consulting his watch.*) I imagine we can make it by midnight.

GABBY. You'll have to step. What kind of car you driving?

CHISHOLM. (*Lighting cigar.*) Duesenberg.

SQUIER. Good-bye, Miss Maple.

GABBY. Just a minute, Alan. (*She turns again to* CHISHOLM.) Excuse me, sir.

CHISHOLM. What?

GABBY. Would you have room in your car for another party? (SQUIER *signals to her not to bother.*)

CHISHOLM. (*Suspicious.*) Who is it?

GABBY. This friend of mine, Mr. Squier. He's on his way to the coast and he—he hasn't got a car just now. He's an author.

CHISHOLM. (*To* SQUIER.) Have you any luggage?

SQUIER. Just this, sir—on my back. (CHISHOLM *looks him over, goes to open door, and calls "Joseph."*)

CHISHOLM. Where'd you come from?

SQUIER. From Saint Tropez. That's on the Riviera. (JOSEPH *comes in.*)

CHISHOLM. I know where it is. Do you think it's all right to give

33

this man a lift to Phoenix? (JOSEPH *subjects* SQUIER *to extremely critical inspection.*)

SQUIER. You've been there?

CHISHOLM. Yes . . . (JOSEPH *taps* SQUIER *all over for concealed weapons.*)

SQUIER. It's a lovely spot, Saint Tropez.

CHISHOLM. (*Without enthusiasm.*) Yes.

JOSEPH. I guess he's all right, Mr. Chisholm.

CHISHOLM. Very well. (JOSEPH *touches his cap and goes out.*) Glad to have you with us.

SQUIER. Thank you very much, Mr. Chisholm. (GABBY *punches* "*No Sale*" *key and takes out a silver dollar.* SQUIER *crosses to her.*) And thank you, Miss Maple. I'll remember your kindness.

GABBY. I forgot to give you your change. (*She offers him the dollar.*)

SQUIER. Oh, no—I wanted you to keep that.

GABBY. (*Pointing to a sign.*) Tipping is un-American and we don't allow it. Here—take it.

SQUIER. I—I can't very well pretend that I don't need . . .

GABBY. Perhaps Mr. Chisholm will take you all the way to the coast. When you get there, send me a postcard, with a view of the Pacific Ocean. I like pictures of the sea. (*She has forced coin into his hand . . .* MRS. CHISHOLM *emerges.*)

CHISHOLM. This is Mr.—er ——

GABBY. Squier.

CHISHOLM. Mr. Squier, darling. We're giving him a lift as far as the Phoenix Biltmore. (MRS. CHISHOLM *frowns.*) It's all right; Joseph went over him.

SQUIER. How do you do, Mrs. Chisholm?

MRS. CHISHOLM. How do you do? Are we ready to start? (*She crosses toward door.*)

CHISHOLM. Just been waiting for you. Come along, Mr. Squier. (*The* CHISHOLMS *have gone out.*)

SQUIRE. I suppose I'll never see you again.

GABBY. No. That's the way it is in a gas station. They come and they go.

SQUIER. But, somehow or other, I'll repay that dollar. God knows when.

GABBY. Perhaps we'll run into each other some day in Bourges. (*The horn of the Duesenberg is heard summoning, shrilly.*)

SQUIER. Good-bye, Gabrielle.

GABBY. (*Shaking hands.*) Good-bye, Alan. (*He goes out. After a moment, she comes down and picks up the Poems of François Villon. Car is heard starting and charging off into the night. GABBY suddenly remembers Neon sign, goes to a switch by door and turns it on. BOZE comes in.*)

BOZE. Well—I took pity on that poor panhandler. I slipped him a dime.

GABBY. You *did?*

BOZE. I tried to—but he wouldn't take it. He said, "I don't deserve your kindness," and handed it back. It's a funny thing about a guy like that: he'll hold you up for a meal and think nothing of it. But when it comes to taking money, they suddenly discover they've got some pride.

GABBY. I appreciate that very much, Boze.

BOZE. Appreciate what, honey?

GABBY. Your wanting to help him. That was very kind.

BOZE. Why, say—you talk as if you were nuts about him.

GABBY. I'm not nuts about him. But now and then you see somebody that's just a natural object of charity.

BOZE. (*Pleased.*) Well! If you appreciate it so much—how about being a little nice to me for a change? (*He goes to her and takes hold of her arms.*)

GABBY. I'd like to be nice to you . . . I'd like to be nice to everybody.

BOZE. You can be, Gabby. Listen—how about us taking a little walk around the Mesa? It's warm out and the moon's just coming up. How about it, sweetheart?

GABBY. But supposing a car came along wanting something?

BOZE. You know there's practically no traffic at this time of night.

GABBY. But suppose someone *did* come . . .

BOZE. Well—what if they did? In a pinch, the old man and that Mexican woman could take care of 'em. And you know how your grandfather is—he'd never notice anything peculiar about us being out for a while. . . . (*He goes after her.*) Listen, honey sweet. You've got to grow up sometime. And before you can grow up, you've got to stop being afraid.

GABBY. I'm not afraid!

BOZE. Oh, yes, you are. You think I'm something terrible and you've got to keep away from me. But I'm not so bad, Gabby

35

I'm just a big guy with a good heart and plenty of hot blood. And I'm full of love, honey. (*He takes her in his arms.*) And so are you. You don't know it yet—but you are. And when we get out there in the moonlight, you'll be glad I suggested it. Honestly you will, honey sweet. (*He kisses her lips passionately. After a moment, she struggles a little. He relaxes his hold on her. He is confident of progress.*) All right—I'm not holding you against your will. I'm not trying to force you into anything that's wrong.

GABBY. I didn't say you were.

BOZE. (*Follows her.*) It isn't wrong—except in the minds of old cranks that have forgotten how to love—if they ever knew. My God! It's the most natural thing in the world, for two people, like us, that are young, and clean, and . . . Why, it'd be wrong if we didn't take the chance when we've got it.

GABBY. Do you know what he said?

BOZE. What who said?

GABBY. He said we'd been trying to fight Nature, and we thought we'd licked it, because we've built a lot of dams, and cellophane and things like that. But that's where we're wrong, and that's what's the matter with the world. We've got to admit that Nature can't be beaten!

BOZE. Well—isn't that exactly what I've been trying to tell you all along?

GABBY. I guess it is, Boze. (*He takes her in his arms again.*)

BOZE. You're coming with me, aren't you, sweetheart? You're going to find out things about Nature more wonderful and exciting than anything you ever dreamed of. Aren't you, honey sweet?

GABBY. Oh, well—what the hell! I'll go out with you, Boze. (*He kisses her.*) We'd better go now.

BOZE. Yes, Gabby. Oh, God—you're a beautiful kid! (*He kisses her again, passionately. A car is heard stopping. They break apart, quickly.*) I'll get rid of 'em fast. (*He starts toward door, but stops short when it opens and JACKIE appears. He is a short, chubby, cherubic gangster. He carries a sub-machine-gun and wears a cheery smile.*)

JACKIE. Now—just behave yourselves, folks, and nobody'll get hurt. Who's the boss here?

BOZE. He's out.

JACKIE. Got any guns with you? (*He searches BOZE with practiced speed.*)

BOZE. No. (*He and* GABBY *have been retreating into the room as* JACKIE *has advanced. Following* JACKIE *has come* RUBY, *thin, sallow, adenoidal—and after him has come* DUKE MANTEE—*well-built but stoop-shouldered, with a vaguely thoughtful, saturnine face. He is about thirty-five and, if he hadn't elected to take up banditry, might have been a fine leftfielder. There is, about him, one quality of resemblance to* ALAN SQUIER; *he too is unmistakably condemned. He is hatless and unshaven and wears an ill-fitting suit with a gray prison shirt.* MANTEE *carries no visible arms; but* RUBY *has another machine-gun and a sawed-off shot-gun.*)

JACKIE. This is Duke Mantee, folks. He's the world-famous killer and he's hungry. (DUKE *looks around.*)

DUKE. What's in there and in there? (*He speaks quietly, even gently, with an effortless ferocity.*)

GABBY. That's the kitchen, and in there's our bedrooms.

DUKE. You two married?

GABBY. No. He just works here.

JACKIE. Anybody else in?

BOZE. Only one old man and . . .

GABBY. My grandfather's in there and the cook. There's nobody in there.

DUKE. Bring 'em in, Jackie.

JACKIE. O. K., Duke. (*He goes out at upper* L. DUKE *goes to front door and calls out.*)

DUKE. Hey, Pyles. (PYLES' *voice is heard to reply:* "*Yeah, boss.*") Back that car into the shadow and stay with it.

PYLES' VOICE. Do I get to eat?

DUKE. You'll eat. (DUKE *goes to table, downstage* R., *and takes his coat off, revealing a harness over his waistcoat with two revolvers in holsters under either arm-pit. He folds his coat neatly and lays it on bench, then turns to* RUBY.) Hey, Ruby—pull that table over here. (RUBY *moves table to* R. *as directed.* BOZE *lowers his hands.*) Keep 'em up. (*The hands go up promptly.* RUBY *picks up his machine-gun.*) Take a look around in there.

RUBY. How long do we stay here?

DUKE. Until they get here.

RUBY. You're going to wait for that blonde?

DUKE. Get out!

RUBY. O. K. (*He goes out at lower* L.)

DUKE. You sit down there. (BOZE *sits down as directed at* C. *table.*) What have you got to eat, sister? (GABBY *produces menu card.* DUKE *addresses* BOZE.) Football player, eh?

BOZE. Yes. And you better not let me get close enough to take a sock at you.

DUKE. (*Unconcerned.*) I used to be quite a fan. What's your school?

BOZE. Nevada Tech.

DUKE. Never heard of it. (GRAMP *and* PAULA *the cook come in from kitchen, followed by* JACKIE.)

PAULA. Don't shoot me, mister. Don't kill me, mister. In the name of the Holy Mother of God, don't kill me, mister. (JACKIE *prods her with machine-gun. She screams lustily.*)

JACKIE. Quiet, Pepita—quiet. We aren't going to do you any harm. (*In a ludicrously soothing voice.*) All we're going to do is ask you to cook something. You wouldn't mind that, would you, Pepita?

PAULA. No, mister. I swear to God, I cook anything. You just tell me . . .

JACKIE. All right, Pepita. We got that settled.

GRAMP. (*Staring admiringly at* DUKE.) So you're Mantee, are you? You're the killer!

DUKE. Would you mind sitting down over there, Pop? Take a look around that counter, Jackie. (GRAMP *sits down at* L. JACKIE *searches counter.*)

JACKIE. Yes, Pop. That's the greatest killer alive today. Did you hear what happened in Oklahoma City? (DUKE *inspects menu.*)

GRAMP. Yes—I heard. You pulled off a massacre.

JACKIE. Who said it was a massacre? (*He comes down from counter.*)

GRAMP. The Denver Post. (*He holds up paper.*)

JACKIE. (*Snatching it.*) Let me see it!

DUKE. Put that paper down! (JACKIE *drops paper.*)

JACKIE. Did it say how many we killed?

GRAMP. Six killed and four wounded.

JACKIE. Did you hear that, Duke? We killed six and wounded four. (*He returns to counter to empty cash register.*)

DUKE. (*To* GABBY.) Got any steak?

GABBY. Only hamburger.

PAULA. And we got chicken, mister.

38

GRAMP. Two of the wounded's not expected to live.

DUKE. All right. Cook the chicken and four hamburgers. And plenty of onions.

JACKIE. Boy! That was some massacre!

GABBY. Anything else? (RUBY *comes in from lower* L.)

RUBY. Nobody in there, boss. There's a good window at the end of the hall with a four-foot drop to the ground, right by where the car is.

DUKE. Take a look around outside. Tell Pyles not to hit that horn unless somebody comes up that really looks like trouble, and then to hit it plenty. (RUBY *goes out.*) Bring us beer for the bunch, sister. (*He addresses* BOZE *and* GRAMP.) You fellers like to join us?

BOZE. I never touch it.

GRAMP. I guess I'll have whiskey.

GABBY. (*To* GRAMP.) No, none for you, Gramp.

GRAMP. (*Disconsolate.*) She says I can't have even a little one.

DUKE. Let him have it, sister.

JACKIE. Sure! He can only be young once.

PAULA. Can I begin cooking now, mister?

DUKE. Yeh. Go with her, Jackie. (RUBY *returns.*)

JACKIE. Come on, Pepita. And while the chicken's in the oven, you and me'll have a little fun, eh, kid? (*They go out into kitchen.*)

DUKE. Hey, Ruby. Sit down there. (RUBY *sits down between counter and front door.*) And keep that gun in your lap. (RUBY *obeys, and from now on his eyes ceaselessly patrol the area from front door to kitchen door.* DUKE *crosses with a convict's gait and goes out at the* L. GABBY *is behind counter getting out the beer.* GRAMP *rises and starts to cross to his rocking chair.*)

RUBY. Sit down!

GRAMP. (*Sitting down hastily.*) You needn't think I'm scared of you. I've known *real* killers in my time. And they knew how to make a six-shooter act like a machine-gun. Did you ever hear of fanning?

RUBY. No.

GRAMP. Well—you'd file down the trigger catch so that the hammer worked free, and then you'd fan it like this. (*He points his forefinger at* RUBY *and wiggles his thumb.*) Wild Bill Hickock once knocked over five men that way. They was lined up at a bar and . . . (SQUIER *comes in, hatless and breathless.* GABBY *is in* C. *of stage, with tray of bottles and glasses of beer.*)

GABBY. Alan! What did you come back for?

SQUIER. (*Panting.*) There are some bandits around here.

BOZE. Yes. So we heard.

SQUIER. They cut in ahead of us about a mile down the road, and made us stop and get out, and then they got into Mr. Chisholm's car and drove off. They said we could take their car, but they'd left it locked. They were terrible-looking cut-throats, with a lot of guns and ammunition. (*He addresses* BOZE.) Could you come with me back there and see if you can unlock that . . . (DUKE *comes in from* L.)

GABBY. Look out, Alan! (SQUIER *turns and sees* DUKE. *Then he looks around and sees* RUBY *who has raised his machine-gun.*)

SQUIER. (*Lamely.*) Oh—so we—meet again.

DUKE. Sit down, pal. Down there.

SQUIER. Why, thanks, I'd be delighted to.

DUKE. Wait a minute. (*He takes the rucksack from* SQUIER, *who then sits down opposite* BOZE *at* C. *table.*)

GRAMP. (*Proudly.*) That's Duke Mantee. We were looking at his picture. Remember?

SQUIER. Yes—I remember. (DUKE *goes to extreme* R. *and sits down, his back to wall.*)

DUKE. Join us in a glass of beer?

SQUIER. Why—thank you—but might I have some whiskey, instead?

DUKE. Certainly. Give him a drink, sister. And how about turning on the radio? (GABBY *puts bottle and a glass before* SQUIER. *He pours himself a stiff one.*)

GRAMP. What did I tell you? Look at that chin. He's a killer, all right!

BOZE. He's a gangster and a rat!

SQUIER. Sh!

GRAMP. *He* ain't a gangster! He's a real old-time desperado. Gangsters is foreigners. He's an American! And if the sheriffs find out he's here, we'll see some real killing—*won't* we? (GABBY *turns on radio. Soft, sticky music emerges.*)

DUKE. The cops ain't likely to catch up with us—not tonight. So we can all be quiet and peaceable, and have a few beers together, and listen to the music—and not make any wrong moves. Because

40

—I may as well tell you, folks—old Ruby there, with the machine-gun—he's pretty nervous and jumpy and he's got the itch between his fingers. So let's everybody stay where they are.

SQUIER. Let there be killing! All evening long, I've had a feeling of Destiny closing in. (*To* DUKE.) Do you believe in astrology?

DUKE. I couldn't say, pal.

SQUIER. I don't—normally. But just now, as I was walking along that road, I began to feel the enchantment of this desert. I looked up at the sky and the stars seemed to be reproving me, mocking me. They were pointing the way to that gleaming sign, and saying, "There's the end of your tether! You thought you could escape it, and skip off to the Phoenix Biltmore. But we know better." That's what the stars told me, and perhaps they know that carnage is imminent, and that I'm due to be among the fallen. . . . It's a fascinating thought.

DUKE. Let's skip it. (*He lifts his glass.*) Here's happy days.

GRAMP. Yes, sir—it sure is pleasant to have a killer around here again.

SQUIER. Yes. It's pleasant to be back again—among the living.

(*He raises his glass.*) Hooray! (*He drinks.*)

CURTAIN

ACT II

About half an hour has elapsed since the end of Act I.
DUKE *and* JACKIE *are finishing their meal at* R. *table.*
RUBY *is sitting on a stool at counter, drinking coffee,*
watching everything. GRAMP *and* PAULA *are sitting at*
table at L. BOZE *and* SQUIER *are at* C. *The radio is*
murmuring faintly.
GABBY *alone is permitted to move about—removing*
dishes, refilling coffee cups.

GRAMP. That old Andy Anderson I was telling you about, he was
a great character. He didn't kill for business reasons, like you
fellers. He killed just for the fun of it. He was born somewheres
up in Nova Scotia and come down to the State of Maine so's he
could get into the Civil War and he fit all through it. And he
never stopped talking about it as long as he lived. He always said
that was a regular paradise for killing. He'd stick a Johnny Reb
with his bayonet, throw him over his shoulder and then stick another. And he always said that the beauty of it was there was
no sheriffs around to reprove him for it.

JACKIE. Say, Pop—I wish you wouldn't talk so much about blood
while we're eating.

BOZE. Got it on your conscience, eh?

JACKIE. On my *what*?

BOZE. Yes—I thought so. A punk like you hasn't got any more
conscience than a coyote.

JACKIE. Hmm! Listen to the halfback. How much did *you* get for
playing on the team?

BOZE. I worked my way through college!

JACKIE. What were you doing? Peddling subscriptions to The
American Boy?

BOZE. I worked for three whole years in the Student Laundry.

JACKIE. Oh—how *nice!* (*He lifts his coffee cup.*)

BOZE. Wait a minute—smart guy. I got something to show you.

42

(He reaches for his wallet.)

RUBY. Keep your hand off your hip!

BOZE. I was only going to show him a newspaper clipping that said I ought to be All-American. . . . I scared you, did I? I know it. You're all yellow.

(A none too pleasant expression appears in JACKIE'S eyes over the rim of his coffee cup.)

SQUIER. I'd be a little tactful, Boze. Remember—they're your guests. (GABBY *has sat down at* C. *table between* SQUIER *and* BOZE.)

BOZE. They're a bunch of yellow dogs. That's what made 'em turn crooked in the first place.

SQUIER. No—no. Cowardice isn't the cause of crime. It has something to do with glands.

BOZE. They just haven't got the guts to face the bigger problems of life. They've got to fight their way with guns instead of with principles. (SQUIER *is by now slightly tight and is to become more so, by imperceptible degrees, as the Act proceeds.* JACKIE *sets down his coffee cup with ominous deliberateness and rises, picking up a sawed-off shotgun.)*

JACKIE. Step over to that side of the room, halfback.

GRAMP. You're going to kill him?

BOZE. *(Scared.)* It's just what I said . . .

JACKIE. Come on. This shotgun scatters, and you wouldn't want me to hurt that cute dame, would you?

(The dulcet chimes of the radio are heard. BOZE *slowly rises.)*

SQUIER. *(To* JACKIE.*)* You know—you're taking this much too seriously. *(The radio announcer's voice can be heard introducing the nightly news broadcast.)*

BOZE. I'm not afraid to die. *(But his voice is strained.)*

JACKIE. Come on! Move!

DUKE. Step up that radio—will you, sister? *(To* JACKIE.*)* Sit down, Jackie Cooper.

JACKIE. Did you hear what he . . . ?

DUKE. *(Grinning.)* Sit down! *(To* BOZE.*)* You too. *(They both sit down.* GABBY *has turned up volume control dial.)*

RADIO VOICE. *(Very brisk.)* . . . all anxious first off to hear latest bulletins concerning the greatest man-hunt in human history. A

43

monster dragnet has been cast over the entire southwest from St. Louis to the Pacific Coast. National Guardsmen are co-operating with state police and the famed Texas Rangers as well as countless local posses and Legion posts in a determined effort to apprehend the members of the notorious Mantee gang—to bring to justice this fierce, colorful band of murderers, kidnappers, bank-robbers, perpetrators of the shocking massacre in Oklahoma City. . . .

JACKIE. Take a bow, Duke.

RADIO VOICE. The gang made its escape in two cars, one of which contained Mantee and three other men, the other car containing three men and *one woman.* The Mantee car was seen early this morning at Tularosa and later at Hillsboro in New Mexico. The second car was positively identified at Estelline in the Texas Panhandle when it stopped at the local police station, held it up, and departed with a large supply of guns and ammunition.

JACKIE. Nice going, boys! I don't see how they did it with Doris along to . . .

DUKE. Shut up!

RADIO VOICE. Both cars are undoubtedly headed for the border, but it is considered certain they haven't reached it, due to the number and vigilance of the patrols. War-time conditions prevail on all the roads of Western Texas, New Mexico and Arizona and you know how the officers of the law are in this red-blooded frontier region: they shoot first and ask questions afterward.

(JACKIE *indicates his scorn, but* DUKE *withers him with a look.*)

RADIO VOICE. The Governor of Arizona has issued the following statement: "As long as Mantee and his followers are at large a blot of shame will mar the proud scutcheon of these United States. Any citizen who knowingly gives aid or comfort to these public enemies is a traitor to his country and will be answerable before the great bar of public opinion." . . . I'll now give you the scores of the leading football games of the day. Carnegie Tech—13, Miami—7; Washington State—19 . . .

DUKE. Turn it off, sister.

RADIO VOICE. U. S. C.—0; Navy 21, Virginia—6 . . . (GABBY *switches off radio.*)

JACKIE. (*To* PAULA.) Did you hear that, Pepita? You're a traitor for cooking for us. They'll string you up for that—if they can find a tree around here.

PAULA. The Holy Mother of God knows they put a gun in my stomach and said *you cook* . . .

JACKIE. Sure—*she* knows. But that don't count with the Governor. We're Public Enemies.

DUKE. (*To* RUBY.) Go on out to the car, Ruby, and tell Pyles to come in and get his supper. And tell him to bring in that sack of ammunition and the road map. And you stay there and keep awake.

RUBY. Yeah. O. K. (*He goes out.*)

GRAMP. Are you going to make a run for the Border, boys?

JACKIE. Oh, sure! We'll give you our whole route before we leave, so's you can tell the hick cops and have 'em give us a motorcycle escort.

SQUIER. I think I'm about ready for another whiskey, Gabrielle, if I may. (GABBY *goes behind counter and brings forth a quart bottle and a bottle of drinking water, which she places on table.*)

BOZE. Listen, Panhandler! Who told you you could call her by her first name?

SQUIER. Now, please, Boze—you and I must be friends, as long as they'll let us.

JACKIE. Why don't you take a sock at *him*, halfback? He hasn't got a gun. (PYLES *comes in. He is a lean, lithe Negro, who carries a machine-gun and a bulging gunny sack.*)

PYLES. Hi, everybody! 'Bout time you got around to asking me in. Here's your map, boss. (*He puts sack full of ammunition down on a bench at back, and tosses map down on the table before* DUKE.) Lord, God! Look what you done to that chicken!

DUKE. (*To* PAULA.) Cook him some hamburger, sister.

PAULA. All right, mister. (*She rises.*) But you people better tell that mister Governor I didn't . . .

DUKE. Go with her, Pyles.

PYLES. O. K., boss. I guess I don't get to eat with the white folks.

(*He picks up carcass of the chicken and starts to gnaw it as he crosses to kitchen.*)

DUKE. Look around in there and see if you can find any rope.

PYLES. O. K., boss. (*He turns quickly to* DUKE.) When we going to lam out of here?

DUKE. When it's time.

JACKIE. Sure—as soon as the Duke connects with that heavy date.

45

(He winks broadly at PYLES.*)*

PYLES. *(As he goes.)* Well—I don't like that dame stuff. I like to get out of range. *(He has gone out at* L. *after* PAULA. DUKE *has opened Road Atlas to Arizona and New Mexico, and from now on he and* JACKIE *are studying it and murmuring to each other in inaudible tones.)*

GRAMP. How about passing that bottle over this way?

SQUIER. Why, certainly. Forgive me. . . . *(He is reaching for bottle, but* GABBY *stops him.)*

GABBY. No! *(To* GRAMP.*)* You've had all you're going to get.

SQUIER. *(To* GRAMP.*)* I'm very sorry.

GRAMP. Oh—that's all right. *(He reaches in his pocket for his pipe.)*

JACKIE. What are you doing?

GRAMP. Going to smoke my pipe.

DUKE. Go ahead, Pop. *(*GRAMP *takes out pipe, fills it with great care, lights it, and lapses into silence as he sits in his rocking chair.)*

BOZE. How long are you yeggs going to stick around here?

JACKIE. Keep quiet, halfback.

BOZE. The longer the better, to suit me. Because the U. S. Government is after you and pretty soon they'll be sending for your relatives to identify the bodies and it will probably be the first good look at you they've had in years.

GABBY. You'd better do what you're told and keep your trap shut.

SQUIER. That's good advice, Boze. Because those glandular phenomena I was talking about manifest themselves in sudden and violent ways.

BOZE. *(Savagely.)* How are you going to pay for all that liquor you're drinking? *(*BOZE *is in an ugly mood, the result of humiliating frustration, and he is taking it out on the one completely defenseless person present.)*

SQUIER. I can pay, and will pay, Boze. For every drop! I have a dollar.

BOZE. Oh, you *have!* So you were holding out on us when you . . .

SQUIER. No —— No. I've acquired it since then.

BOZE. Where did you get it?

GABBY. Probably those rich people gave it to him. Now lay off!

46

(*Kitchen door opens and* PYLES *appears.*)

PYLES. Here's some clothesline, boss.

DUKE. Throw it down. (PYLES *tosses coil on floor and vanishes into kitchen.*)

BOZE. So you turned down my dime and accepted their dollar. Your pride has its price, eh?

SQUIER. If you must know—I'll tell you the extent of my pride. Gabrielle gave me the dollar.

BOZE. (*To* GABBY.) You *did?*

GABBY. It's none of your God-damn business what I do.

BOZE. You were feeling kind of generous tonight, weren't you? (*He turns to* SQUIER.) Would you like to know what she was just going to give me when those rats showed up? Would you like to know?

GABBY. Well—speaking of rats! Of all the low, slimy, stinking . . .

SQUIER. No, Gabby. You mustn't blame Boze for anything he says now. He's a man of muscle, and he's suffering from the pangs of frustration.

GABBY. I say, you're a dirty, low, stinking . . .

BOZE. I didn't mean it, Gabby.

GABBY. Then why the hell did you start . . . ?

BOZE. I'm terribly sorry, honey sweet. They've got me absolutely crazy mad, with those shotguns and machine-guns staring me in the face.

SQUIER. That's all it is.

BOZE. I didn't know what I was saying. Will you please forgive me, Gabby?

GABBY. No! Never!

BOZE. (*Humbly.*) All right.

SQUIER. I sympathize with you utterly, Boze. Did you ever read "All Quiet on the Western Front"?

BOZE. No.

SQUIER. Well—all of us here tonight are under very much the same tension. You'd better have a drink, old man. (*He has one himself.*)

BOZE. (*Ignoring* SQUIER.) I love you, Gabby. (*Startled by this sudden declaration* SQUIER *sets down his glass.*) I love you, sweetheart—and if I thought I'd done or said anything to hurt you,

47

I'd go over and I'd hang one on those yeggs and die for it, gladly. *Please* tell me you forgive me, honey sweet.

SQUIER. Excuse me. (*He stands up.*) Would you rather I left?

JACKIE. Stay where you are!

SQUIER. But I'm intruding.

JACKIE. Sit down. (SQUIER *sits.*)

GABBY. That's all right, Alan. We've got nothing to hide. Have we, Boze?

BOZE. No—worse luck.

GABBY. (*To* SQUIER.) I told you he'd been trying to make me.

BOZE. Now, listen . . .

GABBY. And tonight, just after you left, he went at it again. And I decided I was ready to give it to him, and find out what it's like.

BOZE. That's a dirty trick—telling that, before a total stranger.

SQUIER. (*To* BOZE.) Honestly, Boze—I'm not blaming you—not for an instant.

GABBY. (*To* BOZE.) I'll say this much for you: you're a pretty good lovemaker when you get going.

BOZE. I wasn't turning on any act. I told you I was full of love, and I was telling the truth, and I don't care who knows it.

(JACKIE *has risen and started to cross toward* L. *with map.*)

JACKIE. Full of love, are you, halfback?

DUKE. And don't let that Mexican hear you mention the names of any of those towns.

JACKIE. I'll be careful, Duke. I don't want to die. I got a dame, too. (*To* BOZE.) Keep it up, halfback. I'm rooting for you. *Touchdown!* (*He goes into kitchen.*)

BOZE. (*To* GABBY.) It doesn't make any difference to you what I'm trying to tell you—because you don't know what it means to be really crazy about somebody. (*She looks at him, through him, for a moment.*)

GABBY. For all you know, maybe I do.

BOZE. I don't believe it. Who have you ever . . . ?

DUKE. Get me a cigar, will you, sister?

GABBY. (*Rising.*) We've got Admiration, White Owl, and Texas Dandies.

DUKE. Whatever costs the most. (GABBY *has gone back of counter to get a cigar box, which she takes down to* DUKE.)

GRAMP. You fellers going to spend the night here?

DUKE. Can't say, Pop. Maybe we'll decide to get buried here. (GABBY *hands him box of cigars and he takes a fistful.*) Thanks.

SQUIER. You'd better come with me, Duke. I'm planning to be buried in the Petrified Forest. I've been evolving a theory about that that would interest you. It's the graveyard of the civilization that's been shot from under us. It's the world of outmoded ideas. Platonism—patriotism—Christianity—romance—the economics of Adam Smith—they're all so many dead stumps in the desert. That's where I belong—and so do you, Duke. For you're the last great apostle of rugged individualism. Aren't you?

(DUKE *has been calmly defoiling a cigar, biting the end off, and lighting it.*)

DUKE. Maybe you're right, pal.

SQUIER. (*Returning to his drink.*) I'm eternally right. But what use do I make of it?

DUKE. I couldn't say.

BOZE. (*To* GABBY, *who is resuming her seat.*) Who were you ever crazy about?

GABBY. Is it any of your business?

BOZE. Everything about you is my business!

GABBY. Well—if you've got to know—it's him.

SQUIER. (*Startled.*) What?

GABBY. I was just telling Boze that I'm crazy about you.

BOZE. That panhandler?

GABBY You don't know the worst of him. He's more than a panhandler. He's a gigolo.

BOZE. Did you ever see him before?

GABBY. No. But that doesn't matter. I love him. I don't think I'll ever love anybody else.

SQUIER. Can I possibly be drunk?

GABBY. You will be if you keep hitting that rye.

BOZE. How did you happen to get that way, Gabby?

GABBY. I don't know. Just something.

SQUIER. I swear before God, Boze—I wasn't trying to be seductive.

BOZE. (*Scornfully.*) No—I don't believe you could even try.

GABBY. After you left, Alan—I felt as if something had been taken out of me—or sort of as if I'd come out of a dream. I caught on to myself, and I knew I'm just another desert rat, and I'll never

49

be anything else. I'd better get rid of all the girlish bunk that was in me, like thinking so much about going to France, and Art, and dancing in the streets. And I'd better make the most of what I can find right here—and it happened to be you, Boze. Do you know what I asked him? I asked him to let me go away with him, and live in sin. (*She turns again to* SQUIER.) But you wouldn't have done it, even if we'd had the money—would you, Alan? (SQUIER *is looking straight into her eyes.*) Would you?

SQUIER. No, Gabrielle.

GABBY. (*To* BOZE.) You see—he doesn't give a hoot in hell for me. I saw that, plainly enough. And it only made me love him all the more. And that's why I was willing to go out into the moonlight with you, when Duke Mantee came in.

DUKE. I'm sorry, sister. I don't like to interfere with anybody's fun.

BOZE. (*With labored insincerity.*) Oh—that's all right. It was probably all for the best.

DUKE. Yes. When I look at you, I guess it was. (DUKE *turns and opens window at his side about three inches.*)

SQUIER. (*Still looking at* GABBY.) I'm sorry now that I came back.

(BOZE *has darted a look at* DUKE, *and there is born in his mind an idea: by a sudden, tiger-like leap, he might get possession of shotgun which is lying on table.*)

BOZE. I'll take a drink of that stuff. (GABBY *passes him bottle which has remained on table.* BOZE *pours himself a stiff one, drinks it—and a moment later pours and consumes another. But he is constantly, furiously watching* DUKE.)

SQUIER. (*Still looking at* GABBY.) When I went out before—it was the poignant ending to a—an idyllic interlude. But now it's spoiled. I can't go forth quite so gracefully again.

GABBY. You're sorry you heard the real truth?

SQUIER. I told you that I'm the type of person to whom the truth is always distasteful.

GABBY. That wife of yours must have been terrible.

SQUIER. Why do you think so?

GABBY. Because she's talked all the heart out of you. I could put it back, Alan.

SQUIER. (*With sudden irritability.*) No! Don't delude yourself. If you have love, and don't know what to do with it, why don't you

50

lavish it on Duke Mantee? There's your real mate—another child of Nature.

GABBY. You'd better not drink any more of that rye.

SQUIER. It's not the rye! It's the same disease that's afflicting Boze! Impotence! (*He stands up.*)

DUKE. Sit down, pal.

SQUIER. What do you care whether I sit or stand? What can I do to assail your superiority?

DUKE. I got to think about my health, pal.

SQUIER. If I had a machine-gun, I wouldn't know what to do with it. . . . I want to talk to him. (*Indicating* GRAMP.)

GRAMP. Me?

DUKE. You can talk sitting down. I heard you doing it.

SQUIER. (*Sitting down.*) Very well . . .

GRAMP. What's on your mind?

SQUIER. Those Liberty Bonds of yours, buried in Santa Fé.

GRAMP. (*Sharply.*) How do *you* know about them?

SQUIER. What are you going to do with them?

GRAMP. Going to leave 'em where they are!

SQUIER. Yes—leave them where they are! Your granddaughter is stifling and suffocating in this desert when a few of your thousands would give her the chance to claim her birthright.

GRAMP. Yes—and maybe give *you* the chance to steal it. I've heard what you've been saying.

SQUIER. That's a low way to justify your stinginess. Oh—I know you were a pioneer once. But what are you now? A mean old miser, hanging on to that money as though it meant something. Why in God's name don't you die and do the world some good?

GRAMP. Must be drunk.

DUKE. (*Rising menacingly.*) Yes—drunk—or just about the lowest-grade son of a bitch I ever run across. What do you mean talking to an old man like that? (RUBY *appears in door.*)

RUBY. Say—there's three people coming down the road. Two men and a woman. Look to me like the owners of that Duesenberg.

DUKE. O. K. Keep quiet when they get here.

RUBY. It's all right out here. You can see plain in the moonlight. It's kind of nice to look at, too. (*He goes out.*)

SQUIER. I admit it, Duke. I was guilty of bad taste—and I apologize, Mr. Maple.

GRAMP. Sure.

51

DUKE. You'd better crawl, or I might have to put the lug on you. Talking to an old man like that . . .

SQUIER. Listen, Duke. If you had any of Robin Hood in you you'd go to Santa Fé, and rob that bank, and give it to her, before it's too late for her to use it as it should be used . . .

GRAMP. She'll get it when she needs it—when she has a family of her own to support—and probably a good-for-nothing unemployed husband . . . (DUKE *turns to look out window.* BOZE *sees his chance.* He *effects the tiger-like leap, seizes shotgun and wrests it from* DUKE'S *frantic grasp.* BOZE *backs away quickly, covering* DUKE.)

BOZE. (Breathless with excitement.) Put 'em up! Now I've got you. I've been waiting for this chance. I've been watching every move you . . . (MR. *and* MRS. CHISHOLM *appear in doorway, followed by* JOSEPH. *Seeing* BOZE *with shotgun, and* DUKE *with hands up,* MRS. CHISHOLM *screams.* BOZE *whirls to cover them. As he does so,* DUKE *whips out one of his revolvers and fires.* BOZE *drops shotgun and grabs his* L. *hand with his* R. *Kitchen door flies open and* JACKIE *hurtles out.*)

DUKE. Get that gun. (*As* JACKIE *dives for shotgun, the* CHISHOLMS *turn to rush into the night.* PYLES *has followed* JACKIE *out of kitchen, his machine-gun at the alert, his mouth full.*)

RUBY'S VOICE. (*From off* R.) Get back there or I'll shoot you dead!

GABBY. Are you hurt, Boze?

DUKE. (*To* JACKIE.) Give me that Tommy. (JACKIE *gives his machine-gun to* DUKE. MR. *and* MRS. CHISHOLM *and* JOSEPH *return, followed by* RUBY.)

BOZE. He got me in the hand. (*His* L. *hand is seen to be covered with blood.*)

JACKIE. So you tried to be brave, did you?

DUKE. Frisk 'em, Ruby. (RUBY *hurriedly taps the* CHISHOLMS *all over.*)

MRS. CHISHOLM. Let us out of here! We didn't have anything to do with this.

JACKIE. Shut up.

MRS. CHISHOLM. I *won't* have that man pawing me.

DUKE. Get back to the car, Ruby.

RUBY. They're harmless, Duke. (*He goes.*)

DUKE. Sit down over there. Come on! Step! You down there.

(*The* CHISHOLMS *sit at the center table, with* SQUIER. JOSEPH *sits upstage by the counter.*) Take him in and bandage him, sister. He'll be all right. Go with 'em, Jackie—and you better take that line and tie him up and leave him in there.

(GABBY *and* BOZE *cross toward the* L.)

JACKIE. (*Picking up the clothesline.*) I'll tie him.

BOZE. (*To the* CHISHOLMS.) God damn you! Why did you have to pick that moment to come in here?

CHISHOLM. Why indeed!

GABBY. Come on, Boze.

BOZE. Oh, God! I had the chance and I muffed it. I could have got Mantee and got him good.

JACKIE. Tough luck, halfback. You made a nice try.

(GABBY *and* BOZE *go out at the* L. *followed by* JACKIE.)

PYLES. Say, boss—we better lam out of here.

DUKE. We go when I say so.

PYLES. (*Contemplating the* CHISHOLMS.) But if any more people come in here we'll have to be sending out for recruits. (*Turns to* JOSEPH.) Hi-yah, colored brother!

JOSEPH. (*With dignified asperity.*) Good evening.

DUKE. Finish your supper, Pyles.

PYLES. Sure you don't need me? They almost got you that time.

DUKE. Almost ain't good enough. Go on.

PYLES. O. K., boss. (*He goes out into kitchen.*)

GRAMP. Say, Mantee—did you mean to hit him in the hand or was that a bad shot?

DUKE. (*Quietly.*) It was a bad shot, Pop. But I had to get it off fast. Now, listen—I let that mugg make a mugg out of me. But— don't anybody try that again. Just keep in mind that I and the boys are candidates for hanging, and the minute anybody makes the wrong move, I'm going to kill the whole lot of you. So keep your seats. (*He returns his revolver to its bolster, picks up Tommy gun and sits down at* R. *There is a dead pause.*)

CHISHOLM. Are you Mantee?

DUKE. Yes, pal.

MRS. CHISHOLM. I knew it was a mistake to take that hitchhiker into the car.

CHISHOLM. I don't see what he had to do with it.

MRS. CHISHOLM. He certainly didn't help matters much. (SQUIER *was at first stunned by* BOZE'S *spectacular action—then, as he thought it over, resentful—and then, as he thought still more, determined to do something spectacular himself. He has helped himself to another stiff slug of rye.)*

SQUIER. *(Gravely.)* I'm afraid that's unanswerable, Mr. Chisholm. I have not helped matters at all—up to now. *(He finishes his drink and turns to* DUKE.) Would you mind passing me that rucksack that's on the bench beside you?

DUKE. What do you want with it?

SQUIER. I want to get out my life-insurance policy. If you reach in there, you'll find it, in a bundle of papers. *(DUKE reaches with his L. hand and extracts the papers.)*

GRAMP. What do you want with your insurance? Expecting to die?

SQUIER. You've guessed it, Mr. Maple. *(DUKE tosses bundle to* SQUIER.) Thank you. Now can I take out my fountain pen? Here it is. *(He points to his breast pocket.* DUKE *nods.* SQUIER *takes out his pen, and starts to write on policy.)*

CHISHOLM. *(To* DUKE.) What about my car?

DUKE. That's a nice bus you got there.

CHISHOLM. Are you going to restore it to me? And my luggage . . .

DUKE. You're likely to get the car back. Let's hope it won't be all full of bullet holes and blood.

MRS. CHISHOLM. There's one little travelling case with some—some things I need. Can I please have that?

DUKE. I took a look in that case.

MRS. CHISHOLM. You're going to steal it?

DUKE. Yes, ma'am. I got a friend that likes rubies.

MRS. CHISHOLM. You're a filthy *thief!*

DUKE. Yes, ma'am.

CHISHOLM. Look here, old man. How much will you take to let us out of here?

DUKE. How much have you got?

CHISHOLM. I could let you have—say—two hundred dollars in cash.

DUKE. Bring it here. *(CHISHOLM walks timorously over to* DUKE, *produces his wallet and starts to take out some bills.)* Just put down the whole wallet. *(CHISHOLM does so, with trembling hands.)* Got any more?

54

CHISHOLM. (*Patting his pants pockets.*) Only some small change.

DUKE. Keep it.

MRS. CHISHOLM. (*Rising.*) Now can we go?

DUKE. No.

CHISHOLM. But I understood that you . . .

DUKE. Sit down where you were.

MRS. CHISHOLM. You are a cheap, contemptible, crooked thief . . .

CHISHOLM. Be quiet, Edith. (*He resumes his seat.*) We're in his hands. There's nothing we can do—but hope that someday the United States Government will take some measures to protect the lives and property of its citizens. (DUKE *has been calmly taking all the money from wallet.*)

DUKE. Here's your wallet, pal. (*He tosses it to* CHISHOLM, *who stoops to pick it up.* SQUIER *has finished writing. He turns to* DUKE *and from now on speaks rapidly and with a peculiar earnestness.*)

SQUIER. Duke—I have a great favor to ask of you.

DUKE. Yeah?

SQUIER. I don't think you'll refuse it. Because—you're a man of imagination. You're not afraid to do—rather outlandish things . . .

DUKE. What are you getting at?

SQUIER. This insurance policy—it's my only asset. It's for five thousand dollars—and it was made out in favor of my wife. She's a rich woman, and she doesn't need that money—and I know she doesn't *want* it, from me. I've written on the policy that I want the money paid to Miss Maple—that young lady in there. If Mr. and Mrs. Chisholm will witness my signature, I'm sure it will be all right. My wife would never contest it. She's a good sort—really she is. Well—what I'm getting at is this, Duke: after they've signed, I wish—I'd be much obliged if you'd just—kill me. (DUKE *looks at him levelly.*) It couldn't make any difference to you, Duke. After all, if they catch you they can hang you only once—and you know better than anyone else they already have more than they need against you. And you can't be bothered by any humane considerations. You'd have a hard time finding a more suitable candidate for extermination. I'll be mourned by no one. In fact, my passing will evoke sighs of relief in certain quarters. You see, Duke—in killing me—you'd only be executing the sentence of the law—I mean, natural law—survival of the fittest . . .

55

GRAMP. My God—he *is* drunk!

DUKE. Sure—and having a fine time showing off.

SQUIER. Of course I'm showing off. I'm trying to outdo Boze in gallantry. But is there anything unnatural in that? Boze was ready to sacrifice his life to become an All-American star. And I'm ready to do likewise. (*He addresses the* CHISHOLMS.) Can't you see I mean it?

CHISHOLM. I'm afraid I'm not greatly interested in your whimsicalities.

SQUIER. I don't blame you. But you must remember that this is a weird country we're in. These Mesas are enchanted—and you have to be prepared for the improbable. I'm only asking that you attest to my signature on this . . .

MRS. CHISHOLM. I believe you *do* mean it!

SQUIER. Good for you, Mrs. Chisholm! You're a kindred spirit! I'll bet that you, too, have been thrilled by "A Tale of Two Cities."

MRS. CHISHOLM. You're in love with her, aren't you?

SQUIER. Yes—yes, I suppose I am. And not unreasonably. She has heroic stuff in her. She may be one of the immortal women of France—another Joan of Arc, or Georges Sand, or Madame Curie. I want to show her that I believe in her—and how else can I do it? Living, I'm worth nothing to her. Dead—I can buy her the tallest cathedrals, and golden vineyards, and dancing in the streets. One well-directed bullet will accomplish that. And it will gain a measure of reflected glory for him who fired it and him who stopped it. (*He holds up insurance policy.*) This document will be my ticket to immortality. It will inspire people to say of me: "*There* was an artist, who died before his time!" Will you do it, Duke?

DUKE. (*Quietly.*) I'll be glad to.

SQUIER. Then can I have this signed?

DUKE. Sure.

CHISHOLM. (*To* GRAMP.) Is he by any chance insane?

GRAMP. Don't ask *me*. He's no friend of mine.

MRS. CHISHOLM. Of *course* he's insane. But what of it? (SQUIER *gives her policy and pen.*)

SQUIER. Thank you, Mrs. Chisholm. Please sign where I've written, "Witness this day." (*They start to sign.*) I'm going to entrust this to you, Mr. Maple. And after I—after the Duke has obliged, put it in the hands of some good lawyer for collection. My passport is on that table for identification purposes. Thank you very much. (*As they hand him back policy.*) Here, Mr. Maple. (*He rises and hands policy to* GRAMP.)

DUKE. Let me know when you want to be killed.

SQUIER. Pick your own moment, Duke. Say—just before you leave. (*He strides upstage nervously, aimlessly.*) But I'd prefer to have her think that you did it in cold blood. Will you all please remember that? (PYLES *comes in.*)

DUKE. O. K., pal. But for the time being, you better sit down. You might get to feeling reckless. (SQUIER *sits down.*)

SQUIER. I want to. Now—I think we'd all better have a drink.

MRS. CHISHOLM. Good!

SQUIER. (*To* PYLES.) Would you mind passing glasses to Mr. and Mrs. Chisholm?

PYLES. Sure. (*He goes behind counter for glasses, while* SQUIER *pours himself another.*) Say, boss—let's lam it out of here. I don't like all them big windows. (*He takes glasses down to the* CHISHOLMS.)

DUKE. We got to give them more time.

PYLES. You oughtn't to trust a dame. They probably got lost down there in the Panhandle.

DUKE. They know this country like a book. Doris was the one who picked this place for meeting up.

PYLES. Well—I wish to God she'd show.

DUKE. Where's that cook?

PYLES. She's all right. I locked her up. (PYLES *has been passing glasses around.* GRAMP *has been reading policy carefully. He turns his attention to* PYLES.)

GRAMP. Hey—I'll have a little of that, too.

PYLES. (*Pouring a drink.*) Why—certainly.

DUKE. Don't give it to him, Pyles. The girl says he oughtn't to have it.

SQUIER. Better not, Mr. Maple, we'll all need clear heads for what is to come.

GRAMP. *My* head's never been muddled yet.

PYLES. (*To* JOSEPH.) Here, brother—you better take it.

JOSEPH. Is it all right, Mr. Chisholm?

PYLES. (*Ashamed for his race.*) Listen to him! "Is it all right,

57

Mr. Chisholm?" Ain't you heard about the big liberation? Come on—take your drink, weasel!

CHISHOLM. Go ahead, Joseph.

JOSEPH. Thank you, sir. (PYLES *hands drink to* JOSEPH, *then crosses to* R., *and sits down on bench by* DUKE. GRAMP *has finished inspection of policy and is putting it in his pocket.*)

SQUIER. Do you think it's legal?

GRAMP. Seems so to me. But I'd like to tell you just one thing, my friend.

SQUIER. And what is that, Mr. Maple?

GRAMP. There ain't a woman alive or ever did live that's *worth* five thousand dollars.

SQUIER. And let me tell *you* one thing—you're a forgetful old fool. Any woman is worth everything that any man has to give—anguish, ecstasy, faith, jealousy, love, hatred, life or death. Don't you see—that's the excuse for our existence? It's what makes the whole thing possible, and tolerable. When you've reached my age, you'll learn better sense.

MRS. CHISHOLM. (*To her husband.*) Did you hear that?

CHISHOLM. (*Wearily.*) I heard.

SQUIER. (*To* GRAMP.) That lovely girl—that granddaughter of yours—do you know what she is? No—you don't. You haven't the remotest idea.

GRAMP. What is she?

SQUIER. She's the future. She's the renewal of vitality—and courage—and aspiration—all the strength that has gone out of you. Hell—I can't say what she is—but she's essential to me, and the whole damned country, and the whole miserable world. And please, Mrs. Chisholm—please don't look at me quizzically. I know how I sound.

MRS. CHISHOLM. (*To* SQUIER.) I'm wondering if you really believe all that—I mean, about women? (*She has already had one stiff drink and is about to have another.*)

SQUIER. Of course I do—and there's a man who agrees with me. (*Indicating* DUKE.) Don't you, Duke?

DUKE. I don't know, pal. I wasn't listening.

SQUIER. Then permit me to speak for you. (*He turns again to* MRS. CHISHOLM.) He could have been over the border long ago, and safe—but he prefers to stay here and risk his life. And do you know why?

MRS. CHISHOLM. Why?

SQUIER. Because he has a rendezvous here with a girl. Isn't that true, Duke?

DUKE. Yes, pal—that's it.

MRS. CHISHOLM. (*To* DUKE.) Do you mean to say you never have time for romance?

DUKE. Not much, lady.

SQUIER. Certainly he has! Just like the Knights of the Round Table—between dragons.

DUKE. I guess we're *all* a lot of saps. But I wouldn't be surprised if he was the champion. (*He turns to* SQUIER.) Did you think I was kidding when I said I'd be glad to knock you off?

SQUIER. I hope that neither of us was kidding. Did you think *I* was?

DUKE. I just wanted to make sure.

PYLES. Say! What you talking about?

DUKE. Shut up.

SQUIER. You gave me the idea, Duke, when you called me a low-grade son of a bitch. Forgive me, Mrs. Chisholm. I hope you don't object to that phrase.

MRS. CHISHOLM. Not in the least.

DUKE. I take it back. You're all right, pal. You've got good ideas. I'll try to fix it so's it won't hurt.

SQUIER. (*Raising his glass.*) You're all right, too, Duke. I'd like to meet you again some day. (*He drinks.*)

DUKE. Maybe it'll be soon.

MRS. CHISHOLM. You know—this frightful place has suddenly becomes quite cosy. (*She finishes her second drink.*)

SQUIER. That's my doing, Mrs. Chisholm. You ought to thank me for having taken it out of the realms of reality.

MRS. CHISHOLM. (*Excitedly.*) I'm going to *see* something at last—and after that dreadful dull day looking at cliff dwellings. (*She turns to her husband.*) Do you realize that we're going to be witnesses at *murder*? He's actually going to shoot him . . .

SQUIER. Sh—please be careful, Mrs. Chisholm. (GABBY *comes in from* L., *followed by* JACKIE.) Hello. How's Boze?

GABBY. He'll be all right.

PYLES. Did you tie him up good?

JACKIE. Yeah—in the bathroom. Say, Duke, it's after ten o'clock.

PYLES. Yeah, boss.

DUKE. We'll give 'em a few more minutes.

SQUIER. (*Significantly.*) A few minutes.

DUKE. (*With a slight grin.*) Not so much more time, pal. (JACKIN *wanders out for a visit with* RUBY.)

GABBY. Listen, Gramp—I've got an idea we ought to sell out right away, tomorrow. It's the best chance we'll ever have, because this place is going to get advertised all over the country and people will be flocking here just to see where Duke Mantee stopped. I'll bet Dana Trimble will boost his offer sure. (*She is standing by table at* L.)

GRAMP. (*Significantly.*) You're still aiming to take that trip to France?

GABBY. No—the hell with that! I'm asking you to do it for Dad's sake. Let him get located in Los Angeles—and maybe I'll find that writer with Warner Brothers, and maybe I'll get a job—and then we'll all be rich.

GRAMP. Don't sound likely to me.

GABBY. You can't tell, Gramp. There might be a great future for Dad in the Legion. That's what he wants, and you ought to give him a whack at it.

SQUIER. And would you be content with that?

GABBY. (*Savagely.*) I'm not thinking about myself! I don't care what happens to me.

SQUIER. But you *must* think about yourself. You want to be a great painter, don't you? Then you'll have to get used to being a colossal egoist, selfish to the core.

GABBY. Are you going to give me more advice? You and your talk about Nature? I thought you told me never to listen to you.

SQUIER. I did—but . . .

GABBY. Well, that's all the advice I'm going to take. (*She turns away from him.*)

MRS. CHISHOLM. Do you mind if I speak up, my dear? Perhaps I could tell you some things that . . .

GABBY. What do *you* know about me?

CHISHOLM. Nothing! If I were you, Edith, I'd keep out of . . .

MRS. CHISHOLM. (*Turning on him.*) You haven't the remotest conception of what's inside me, and you never have had and never will have as long as you live out your stuffy, astigmatic life. (*She turns to* GABBY.) I don't know about you, my dear. But I know what it means to repress yourself and starve yourself through

60

what you conceive to be your duty to others. I've been through that. When I was just about your age, I went to Salzburg—because I'd had a nervous breakdown after I came out and I went to a psychoanalyst there and he told me I had every right to be a great actress. He gave me a letter to Max Reinhardt, and I might have played the Nun in "The Miracle." But my family of course started yapping about my obligation to *them*—who had given me everything, including life. At least, *they* called it "life." They whisked me back to Dayton, to take my place in the Junior League, and the Country Club, and the D. A. R.—and everything else that's foul and obscene. And before I knew it, I was married to *this* pillar of the mortgage loan and trust. And what did *be* do? He took my soul and had it stencilled on a card, and filed. And where have I been ever since? In an art metal cabinet. That's why I think I have a *little* right to advise you.

CHISHOLM. (*Closing bis tired eyes.*) Dear God!

MRS. CHISHOLM. You needn't look so martyred! You know perfectly well that until this minute I've never complained. I've managed to play the part of a self-effacing . . .

CHISHOLM. (*His eyes are now open.*) Never complained, eh! Forgive me if I indulge in some quiet, mirthless laughter.

MRS. CHISHOLM. What you've wanted is a wife who's an ornamental cipher. And, God knows—I've tried and tried to be just that . . .

CHISHOLM. When?

MRS. CHISHOLM. I've given you what you wanted—at the cost of my individuality, my self-respect—and—and everything else . . .

CHISHOLM. At the cost of nothing! I suppose you've never come storming into the office and created a scene just when I was straining every faculty to find ways to pay for . . .

MRS. CHISHOLM. (*To* GABBY.) There—my dear!

CHISHOLM. Your insane extravagance . . .

MRS. CHISHOLM. Be quiet! (CHISHOLM *abandons the argument, as is bis wont.* MRS. CHISHOLM *again to* GABBY.) Perhaps you'll understand now what I mean. Profit by my example and realize that perhaps you have something important to give to the world. Don't let them stifle you with their talk about duty. Go to France —and *find* yourself!

GRAMP. Suppose she learns there's nothing there to find?

MRS. CHISHOLM. Even so—it would be better than endless doubt—

61

which has been my portion. (*She pours herself another drink.* GABBY *sits down at* L.)

SQUIER. You know—it's the damnedest thing about this place. There's something here that stimulates the autobiographical impulse. (*To* DUKE.) What kind of life have *you* had, Duke?

DUKE. A hell of a life.

MRS. CHISHOLM. I don't believe it.

DUKE. Why not, lady? (JACKIE *returns and sits on a stool at counter.*)

MRS. CHISHOLM. Because you've had the one supreme satisfaction of knowing that at least you're a real man.

(CHISHOLM *again shuts his eyes.*)

DUKE. Yeh—that's true. But what has it got me? I've spent most of my time since I grew up in jail, and it looks like I'll spend the rest of my life dead. So what good does it do me to be a real man when you don't get much chance to be crawling into the hay with some dame?

MRS. CHISHOLM. (*After a slight, thoughtful pause.*) I wonder if we could find any hay around *here?*

CHISHOLM. (*Past vehemence.*) For the love of God, Edith . . .

JACKIE. Say! What's been going on here?

SQUIER. I'm not sure—but I *think* the Duke has had an offer.

MRS. CHISHOLM. He certainly has! And it was made with all sincerity, too.

PYLES: Now, listen, boss—don't you go getting into no hay with her. Because we got to lam it out of here.

DUKE. Thanks very much, lady. When I get settled down in Mexico, maybe I'll send you a postcard, with my address.

SQUIER. Excuse me, Duke—but how's the time getting along?

DUKE. It's just about up, pal.

SQUIER. (*Turning to* GABBY.) I must talk to you, Gabrielle.

GABBY. You can wait until after they're gone.

SQUIER. I can't wait. I mean—when they go—I go. I have to tell you now that I love you.

GABBY. Now listen, Alan. I got sort of upset by all that blood, and I don't want to . . .

SQUIER. I tell you solemnly that I love you, with all the heart that is left in me.

JACKIE. Are we waiting just to listen to this?

62

MRS. CHISHOLM. He does love you, my dear. He told us so.

SQUIER. Please, Mrs. Chisholm. I'm capable of saying it. (*He turns to* GABBY.) Even if I'm not capable of making you believe that I . . .

GABBY. Don't make a fool of yourself, Alan. They're all staring at you.

SQUIER. I know they are. But you've got to believe it, and you've got to remember it. Because—you see—it's my only chance of survival. I told you about that major artist, that's been hidden. I'm transferring him to you. You'll find a line in that verse of Villon's that fits that. Something about: "Thus in your field my seed of harvestry will thrive." I've provided barren soil for that seed—but you'll give it fertility and growth and fruition . . .

PYLES. Listen, boss—I got a wife and four children.

MRS. CHISHOLM. Be quiet—you black gorilla!

PYLES. What you call me? (*He rises, his machine-gun at the alert.*)

DUKE. She pegged you, all right, Pyles. Sit down! (*Somewhat reluctantly,* PYLES *obeys.*)

SQUIER. You still think I was being comic?

GABBY. No, Alan. I just think that you—you're kind of crazy. And I guess so am I. And that's why I think we'd be terribly happy together. (SQUIER *looks into her eyes.*)

SQUIER. Don't say that, Gabrielle.

GABBY. Why not—when I believe it, with all my heart?

SQUIER. (*After a moment.*) Well—maybe you're right . . .

GABBY. You're beginning to admit it.

SQUIER. Maybe we will be happy together in a funny kind of way.

GABBY. Alan! (*Impulsively, she goes forward and kneels beside him.*)

JACKIE. Hey!

DUKE. Leave 'em alone!

GABBY. Alan! If you're going away, I'm going with you—wherever it is.

SQUIER. (*Taking hold of her hand.*) No, Gabrielle. I'm not going away, anywhere. I don't have to go any farther. Because I think I've found the thing I was looking for. I've found it—here, in the Valley of the Shadow.

GABBY. What, Alan? What have you found?

SQUIER. I can't say what it is, Gabrielle. Because I don't quite know, yet! (*He looks into her eyes for a moment, then turns suddenly to* DUKE.) All right, Duke. We needn't wait any longer.

(*Three sharp toots from the Duesenberg are heard.*)

DUKE. Watch it, boys! (PYLES *and* JACKIE *hastily duck out of range of windows.*)
CHISHOLM. What was that?
JOSEPH. It was our horn, Mr. Chisholm. (JACKIE *is by door,* DUKE *by R. window,* PYLES *is crouched, covering those in the room.*)
JASON'S VOICE. Who's that?
RUBY'S VOICE. Stick up your hands! (DUKE *has levelled his machine-gun through the slightly open window.*)
DUKE. We got you covered by machine-guns. Open that door, Jackie. Come on, boys. Walk in the front door, and keep 'em up! Cover the door, Jackie.
JACKIE. I got it.
DUKE. Come on! Keep coming! (JASON *comes in, followed by two fellow legionnaires—one, the* COMMANDER, *a peppery little man, and another who is burly and stupid. All are in the same gaudy uniforms and all look bewildered.*) Get those guns, Jackie. (JACKIE *systematically disarms legionnaires. He tosses guns into ammunition sack.* RUBY *comes to door.*)
RUBY. All clear out here.
DUKE. Is their car in our way?
RUBY. No—it's a good mask.
DUKE. O. K. Get back to the car. (RUBY *disappears into the night.*)
JASON. Is this a stick-up?
JACKIE. What a guesser!
GRAMP. Say—Jason. That there's Duke Mantee. Been here all evening. He and his gang picked this place out of the whole southwest.
DUKE. What's that uniform you're wearing?
JASON. It's the Ralph M. Kesterling Post of the American Legion.
COMMANDER. I'm the commander of this post, buddy, and I want to tell you that all of us men fought in the World War. You wouldn't shoot us down in cold blood?
JACKIE. (*Cheerfully.*) Sure we would.
DUKE. Sit down, boys.

64

ANOTHER LEGIONNAIRE. (*Very basso.*) Where?

JACKIE. On your cans, Legion.

DUKE. Down there on the floor—in a bunch—and stay there. (*With some little sacrifice of dignity,* LEGIONNAIRES *sit down on floor in a huddle in* C.) Why did you come here?

JASON. This is where I live.

GABBY. That's my father.

DUKE. Why did you bring the whole regiment with you?

COMMANDER. We were trailing you. And by God we caught up with . . .

JASON. Shut up, Commander. The less we talk the better for all concerned.

JACKIE. Some legion! Out gunning for the bad men—and look at 'em now!

DUKE. What made you think I'd be around here?

COMMANDER. They caught your pals.

OTHER. Three men and a blonde.

PYLES. Don't you try to go get 'em out now, boss!

DUKE. Where was it? (*There is no reply.* DUKE *continues with unwonted ferocity.*) Come on—tell me—or I'll tear holes a yard wide in them pansy uniforms!

JASON. They caught 'em at Buckhorn.

DUKE. Where's that? (PYLES *pulls map from his pocket.*)

OTHER. It's in New Mexico—'bout ninety—hundred miles southeast of here.

DUKE. When?

JASON. I don't know.

COMMANDER. We heard about it half an hour ago. Every man in this state that can bear arms has turned out to . . .

PYLES. Here it is, boss. Buckhorn—on Route 11.

JACKIE. How'd they get 'em?

COMMANDER. It was the regular army!

OTHER. Your friends run right into a troop of the U. S. Cavalry.

JASON. I warn you, Mantee—you'd better get out of here, for your own good.

DUKE. Is anybody else coming this way?

JASON. I don't know. I swear to God I don't. But there are posses all around here, and I don't want to get this place shot up.

COMMANDER. You got the whole mighty strength of this nation after you now, buddy.

JACKIE. Listen, Legion—when we're got it will be by *real* cops—not by any overgrown Boy Scouts in fancy dress.

JASON. All right—you can talk big, if you want to. But I'll tell you that the woman in that car has been doing some talking.

DUKE. (*After a moment.*) What?

JACKIE. It was Doris. She snitched. They always snitch!

DUKE. Shut up! (*To* JASON.) What were you saying?

JASON. I'm telling you for your own good, Mantee—they know where you were heading—they've picked up your trail—and they'll get you . . .

JACKIE. She *has* snitched! Come on, Duke!

SQUIER. Don't listen to them, Duke! (SQUIER *is leaning forward, watching* DUKE *with great intentness. He sees that* DUKE, *for once, has been propelled into a state of turbulent, agonized indecision.*)

PYLES. Come on, boss—or we're all dead.

COMMANDER. The law's closing in on you!

JACKIE. What's the matter with you, Duke? Why the hell don't you . . .

DUKE. (*With sudden savagery.*) For Christ's sake, shut up! *Shut up!* Give me time to think.

SQUIER. (*Urgently.*) No, Duke—don't waste any time thinking. That isn't your game. Don't listen to what they're telling you. You've got to keep going and going and going ——

PYLES. Yeah—and go fast.

JACKIE. You've been double-crossed and bitched, and the next thing you'll be laid flat on a marble slab . . .

DUKE. Where'd they take her?

JASON. I don't know. Maybe to Albuquerque.

JACKIE. If we head for there, they'll take *us!*

SQUIER. You want revenge, don't you! You want to go out of your way again to get that blonde who snitched. Don't do it, Duke. Even if she did betray you, don't you commit a worse crime. Don't betray yourself. Go on, run for the border—and take your illusions with you!

JACKIE. He's right, Duke!

DUKE. I told you to shut up! (*He says that to* JACKIE, *but he is looking hard at* SQUIER, *who is talking with passionate earnestness.*)

SQUIER. You know they're going to get you, anyway. You're obso-

66

lete, Duke—like me. You've got to die. Then die for freedom. That's worth it. Don't give up your life for anything so cheap and unsatisfactory as revenge.

PYLES. I hear a car coming, boss. We better lam. (DUKE *looks at* SQUIER *curiously, for a moment.*)

DUKE. All right, pal. I'm going. Now, listen, folks; we've had a pleasant evening here and I'd hate to spoil it with any killing at the finish. So stay where you are until we're out of sight, because we'll be watching. Better cut that phone wire, Jackie. Pack up the ammunition, Pyles. (PYLES *and* JACKIE *are galvanized into action.*)

SQUIER. Wait a minute! You're not forgetting me? (JACKIE *is opening his knife,* PYLES *is picking up ammunition sack, and* DUKE *is covering all, when the Duesenberg horn is heard again.* DUKE, PYLES *and* JACKIE *duck.*)

DUKE. (*Peering out window.*) Car's stopped out in the road. There's a guy with a rifle.

PYLES. Cops?

DUKE. Looks like it.

JACKIE. Hicks or G's?

DUKE. Hicks. Lay low!

COMMANDER. It's the Sheriff! He's got you, Mantee!

JASON. I warned you! You'd better surrender now before they start . . . (*A burst of machine-gun fire is heard from* L.)

PYLES. That's Ruby shooting.

DUKE. The God-damn fool. Get out there to that window, Jackie, and tell him to hold his fire. We don't want 'em drilling that car. (JACKIE *starts to go.*) Wait! Tell him to open up if they try to drift around that side.

JACKIE. O. K. (*Stooped over, he goes to door at lower* L. *and out.*)

JASON. You have no right to endanger the lives of innocent people. You'd better surrender.

DUKE. Get behind that counter, Pyles. And keep this mob in here covered.

PYLES. O. K., boss. (*He crouches on* L. *end of counter.* DUKE *is marvellously alert, crouching by window, muzzle of his gun thrust out.*) What they doing now, boss? (DUKE *delivers a short burst of machine-gun fire out the window.*)

DUKE. They're crawling into the sagebrush the other side of the road. Where are them pans?

PYLES. The sack's right there beside you. (*A shot from outside shatters one of windowpanes.*) Boy—I knowed this place wasn't safe! (*Wails are heard from* PAULA, *off at* L.)

DUKE. You folks better get down. Lie down, all of you, close to gether in the middle. Watch 'em, Pyles.

PYLES. I'm watching! (*All hasten to obey, so that they are lying flat on their stomachs, close together.* JACKIE *returns.*)

JACKIE. O. K., Duke.

DUKE. Where's the light switch?

GRAMP. To the right of the door.

DUKE. Turn 'em out, Jackie. (JACKIE *turns out lights.*)

CHISHOLM. (*To his wife.*) Do you want any hay now? (*The strip of faces and feet of the prone is illumined by the glow of light from door at* R. *Through windows and panes of door come bright moonlight and the green Neon gleam to illumine, dimly,* DUKE *and* JACKIE.)

DUKE. Get to the kitchen door, Jackie. Hold your fire, unless they try to rush it. They'll try to work around that direction to the shadow of that mesa. It's their only cover. When they get around there, we'll lam.

JACKIE. How many are there?

DUKE. Six or seven. Nothing to worry about. (*Another shot from outside.*) When enough of 'em get across that road, give 'em a couple of bursts to scare 'em and then snap back here. And watch yourself, kid!

JACKIE. O. K., Duke. (*He crosses the line of bodies.*)

COMMANDER. Ouch! (*Still another shot from outside breaks a window.* JACKIE *has gone out at* L. BOZE'S *voice can be heard shouting:* "*Let me out of here! Let me out of here!*" PAULA *can be heard wailing prayers and imprecations in Spanish.*)

DUKE. Keeping 'em covered, Pyles?

PYLES. I got 'em, boss! I got 'em! (*The subsequent dialogue is punctuated with shots from outside and bursts from* DUKE'S *Tommy-gun.*)

SQUIER. It's an inspiring moment—isn't it, Gabrielle? The United States of America versus Duke Mantee! (*A volley from* SHERIFF'S *posse and Neon light goes out.*)

JASON. They've absolutely wrecked the Neon!

68

GRAMP. It's them deputies shooting. Probably all drunk.

SQUIER. It almost restores in me the will to live—and love—and conquer.

CHISHOLM. Listen, Edith—if I'm killed . . .

MRS. CHISHOLM. What did you say?

CHISHOLM. I said—if I'm killed—and you're not . . . notify Jack Lavery. He has full instructions.

MRS. CHISHOLM. (*Turning away.*) All right.

COMMANDER. Hey—Mantee . . . you're not going to let 'em rush us, are you? (DUKE *replies with another burst.*)

PYLES. Getting any of 'em, boss?

DUKE. Can't get a good angle on 'em. But they're drifting over—and Jackie'll get 'em.

SQUIER. I feel as if I were sitting on top of a mountain . . . in the middle of Penguin Island. Watching . . . watching the odd little creatures. (MRS. CHISHOLM *starts to hum.*) How do you feel about it, darling?

GABBY. I don't know, Alan. And I don't care.

JASON. I wish to God you'd stop that praying.

MRS. CHISHOLM. I'm not praying—I'm singing. (*By now it is apparent that the attackers have been drifting over, the sound of shots comes more from* L.)

PYLES. Why ain't Jackie shooting?

DUKE. The kid knows what he's doing.

COMMANDER. If you let 'em rush us . . . it'll be a massacre.

GABBY. Alan . . . Alan—when you get to France . . . what do you see first?

SQUIER. Customs Officers.

GABBY. But what's the first real sight you see?

SQUIER. The fields and forests of Normandy and then . . .

GABBY. What, Alan?

SQUIER. And then Paris.

PYLES. I better tell Jackie to open up.

DUKE. Stay where you are.

GABBY. Paris! That's the most marvellous place in the world for love—isn't it?

SQUIER. All places are marvellous.

GABBY. Even here.

SQUIER. Especially here, my darling.

JOSEPH. (*Swaying and chanting.*) Oh, Lord! Oh, Lord! It is the judgment of thy wrath on these thy poor sinful children. (*More wails from* PAULA *and shouts from* BOZE.)

JASON. The next thing you know those gas pumps will be up in flames.

SQUIER. As long as I live—I'll be grateful to the Duke . . .

GABBY. Alan . . . Alan . . . will you please kiss me? (*He kisses her.* DUKE *delivers a final prolonged burst, then turns from window.*)

DUKE. O. K., Pyles. We're pulling out. Get Jackie. (PYLES *ducks into kitchen. The shooting from* L. *is now intense.*)

SQUIER. Oh, Lord —— Now it's going to be all over.

GABBY. (*Clinging to him.*) Not for us, Alan—never ——

PYLES. (*Returning.*) Jackie's got killed.

DUKE. How the hell did he do that?

PYLES. I don't know, boss.

DUKE. Well—we got to leave him. You and you and you and you are coming with us to hang on the running board. We got to have shields. (*He has designated the* CHISHOLMS, JOSEPH *and the two* LEGIONNAIRES.)

CHISHOLM. Me?

MRS. CHISHOLM. All right! All right! I don't care what happens to me now. I don't care a bit!

COMMANDER. For God's sake, Buddy, don't let us get shot down like . . .

JOSEPH. Oh, Lord God of Abraham. Oh, Holy Lord . . .

OTHER LEGIONNAIRE. This is the country I was ready to die for . . . (*The foregoing is all jumbled together.*)

GRAMP. Me, too?

DUKE. No, not you, Pop. Come on, on your feet. Get moving out through that door. They won't shoot at you! You won't none of you get hurt if you keep your hands up and make plenty of noise. Come on—keep moving!

PYLES. And we're in one hell of a hurry. (*He is herding them out. Their hands are up and they are shouting lustily.*)

ALL. Don't shoot —— Don't shoot. For God's sake, buddies, don't shoot!

(DUKE *is in doorway, a crouched silhouette against the moonlit desert. His machine-gun is under his* L. *arm, his revolver in his* R. *hand.*)

70

DUKE. (*To those remaining.*) You'd better stay where you are for a while. Good night, folks.

SQUIER. (*Springing to his feet.*) Duke!

GABBY. Alan! Keep down!

SQUIER. Duke!

DUKE. Do you still want it?

SQUIER. (*Desperately.*) It's no matter whether I want it or not. You've got to . . .

DUKE. O. K., pal. (*He shoots.* SQUIER *spins against lunch counter.* GABBY *screams.*) I'll be seeing you soon. (*He goes.*)

GRAMP. God Almighty! He meant it! (GABBY *rushes to* SQUIER. *There are more wails from* PAULA *and shouts from* BOZE, *but the shooting has stopped.*)

JASON. Keep down! (*The motor of the car is heard starting. Door at* L. *bursts open and* SHERIFF *comes in, holding a rifle. Behind him are* HERB *and two* DEPUTIES, *with rifles, pistols, shotguns.*)

SHERIFF. Where'd they go?

JASON. (*Rising.*) Out there.

HERB. (*Full of enthusiasm and moon.*) Let's get 'em, Sheriff! Come on, fellers—we'll shoot 'em dead! (SHERIFF *starts for door, and bumps into* JASON.)

GABBY. Gramp! Go get Boze. He knows about first aid. (GRAMP *goes out at* L.)

SHERIFF. Get out of my way, you clumsy . . . (SHERIFF *goes out front door, followed by* DEPUTIES *and* HERB. *They take cover, and raise their rifles.*)

JASON. Those are innocent people on the running board! (*He switches on lights.*)

HERB. Never mind 'em. Let's shoot the hell out of 'em! (*He shoots.*)

SHERIFF. God damn! Come on. We'll go after 'em. (*He turns out of sight.*)

VOICE OF ANOTHER DEPUTY. Can't drive that car. The tires are all shot.

SHERIFF'S VOICE. Here's a car we can take.

JASON. Wait a minute. That's my car! You've done enough damage to my property.

HERB'S VOICE. Ah—shut up. (SQUIER *lurches toward* C. *table.* GABBY *steadies him and helps him to slump down into a chair.*)

71

SQUIER. It doesn't hurt—or, at least, it doesn't seem . . . It went into this lung, I think. (*He leans forward on table.*)

GABBY. It's all right, Alan.

SQUIER. It isn't all right, Gabrielle. I'm practically dead.

GABBY. No! Alan! You said you wanted to live.

SQUIER. I know I did . . .

GABBY. And I'll live with you. I will!

SQUIER. (*Looking up at her and smiling, feebly.*) I know I said it. I was blinded, then. But now I can see. . . .

GABBY. (*Shouting.*) Boze! Gramp! Somebody! Come here quick!

SQUIER. They were right, Gabrielle . . . I mean the stars. I had to come all this way—to find a reason . . . Oh,—if people only had guts enough, they'd always find . . . (*He covers his eyes with his hand.*) Death is funny-looking when . . . The Duke—understood what it was—I wanted . . . I hope you'll——— (*His arms are stretched out on table and his head has been sinking until it rests between them.*)

GABBY. What, Alan? What did you say? (*She takes hold of his shoulder and, frantically, shakes him.*) Alan . . . (*He is finally silent. Her lip quivers, but she tightens her face.*) No—don't worry, Alan. I'm not going to be a God-damned cry-baby about it . . . I know you died happy . . . Didn't you, Alan? Didn't you? (*After a moment,* BOZE *comes in, followed by* GRAMP. BOZE'S R. hand is in a blood-stained bandage.*)

BOZE. Are you all right, old kid?

GABBY. I guess he's dead.

GRAMP. Sure he is. Mantee couldn't have missed twice.

BOZE. Damned tough. He was a good guy, at that. (*A wail from* PAULA *is again heard.*) What's that?

GABBY. It's Paula. Go in and let her out. (BOZE *goes out at* L. GRAMP *takes insurance policy from his pocket.*)

GRAMP. Listen, Gabby—here's the funny thing. His life insurance for five thousand berries. He made it out to you, and it looks regular. Said he wanted you to spend it on a trip to France to see your mother. Of course, I don't know if it's collectable, but by God, I'm going to get it to Summerfield in the morning. (*He puts policy back in his pocket.*) He was the damnedest feller I ever did see. (*He turns and crosses to* L. *and sits down in his rocking chair.*) Couldn't make him out. (JASON *comes in quickly.*)

JASON. Mantee let 'em off the car 'bout a quarter of a mile up

72

the road. You can see 'em walking back. (*He sees* SQUIER.) Has he ——

GRAMP. Yep—he's gone.

JASON. (*Removing his cap.*) Poor feller. Well—he died a hero's death. We'll give him an honorable funeral.

GABBY. We'll bury him out there in the petrified f⌐

JASON. *What?*

GABBY. That's what he wanted.

GRAMP. Yes—by God—he said so. (JASON *sto⌐ ⌐p to phone behind counter.*)

JASON. Well, maybe his next of kin will have something to say about that. I've got to 'phone the Sheriff's office. They'll never catch Mantee with my car—unless he wrecks that Duesenberg. . . . Hello —— Hello—get me the Sheriff's office in Morenci. . . . Yeh. . . . (GABBY *is still standing close to* SQUIER, *her hands on his shoulder.*)

GABBY. (*Almost to herself.*)
   "Thus in your field my seeds of harvestry will thrive—
   For the fruit is like me that I set ——"

(BOZE *comes in, from kitchen, laughing.*)

BOZE. Boy—it did me good to see that Jackie in a pool of blood. . . .

GABBY. (*Louder, almost defiantly.*)
   "God bids me tend it with good husbandry:
   This is the end for which we twain are met."

JASON. Hello—who's this? . . . Oh—hello, Ernie. . . .

BOZE. (*Wildly.*) Don't keep staring at him . . .

JASON. Jason Maple. . . . Say—Mantee was here and escaped South in a yellow Duesenberg, Ohio license plate. Sheriff went after him, but you got to watch Route 71 and send out the alarm to watch Route 60. Yes—we had quite some shooting here. . . .
(*During this speech the curtain has fallen.*)

CURTAIN

PROPERTY LIST

Act I

Cash register
Catsup bottles
Paper napkins
Toothpicks
Chewing gum
Various portions hamburgers, pies, coffee
Life-saver rack
Cigars, cigarettes, etc., on lunch counter
Cigarettes and matches
Bottles of beer and glasses
2 newspapers
Coffee boiler
Cigar and matches
Slices of pie, dishes, etc., for same
Money: bills and small change
Thin book
Watch chain with gold football charm
Billfold with old newspaper clippings inside
Heavy walking stick and rucksack
Menu cards
Sam Browne belt and pistol holster
3 or 4 revolvers—2 loaded with blanks
Portrait photograph
Gunny sack

Sheaf of water color paintings (rather small)
Cigar box with several cigars in it
Watch
2 sub-machine-guns and a sawed-off shotgun
Leather harness for a man for carrying 2 revolvers.—The revolvers are in the harness
Service trays
Radio

Act II

Bottle of whiskey and bottle of drinking water
Filled gunny sack
Road map
Pipe with tobacco and matches
Coil of clothesline
Small bundle of various papers, including life-insurance policy
Fountain pen
Money wallet with bills
Pocket knife
One windowpane (to be broken by shot)
5 or 6 rifles, shotguns, revolvers, etc., for Sheriff and deputies
Blood-stained bandage
Telephone on counter